A Runaway Teenager Who Found Freedom

An Inspiring Story Of Faith, Love, And Courage

QUYEN T. HA

Copyright © 2021 by Quyen Ha.

All rights reserved. This book or any portion thereof may not be reproduced or used in any manner whatsoever without the express written permission of the publisher except for the use of brief quotations in a book review.

Publishing Services provided by Paper Raven Books

Printed in the United States of America

First Printing, 2021

Paperback ISBN= 978-1-7368491-0-1
Hardback ISBN= 978-1-7368491-1-8

To the boat people who perished in the unforgiving sea while escaping for freedom and to those who made it to shore.

To my parents, without your sacrifice, inspiration, and love I wouldn't have today.

To my beautiful wife for your endless love.

To my children, Ethan and Peter, you have been given a wonderful life, and I pray that you will make the most of it.

Prologue

I watched my son Peter running around the house and enjoying himself. We were gathered at my mom's home to celebrate her eighty-fifth birthday, cheering her on for her resilience, resolve, and incredible love for her children. We reminisced about what our lives have been in the last thirty years in America. We know that we have been given the greatest gift of all - freedom. One escape from Viet Nam has changed my family tree for generations to come. My son will live in freedom for the rest of his life. The biggest challenge he has to face is to keep America free for his children and his children's children. I remind him daily what my life was without freedom because I want him to understand how precious freedom is. The freedom we have isn't free - someone has to die for it. We thank God for giving us this wonderful life. We thank America for the freedom that she has given us. And we thank the men and women who fought for our freedom, who are fighting for our freedom, and who will fight for our freedom.

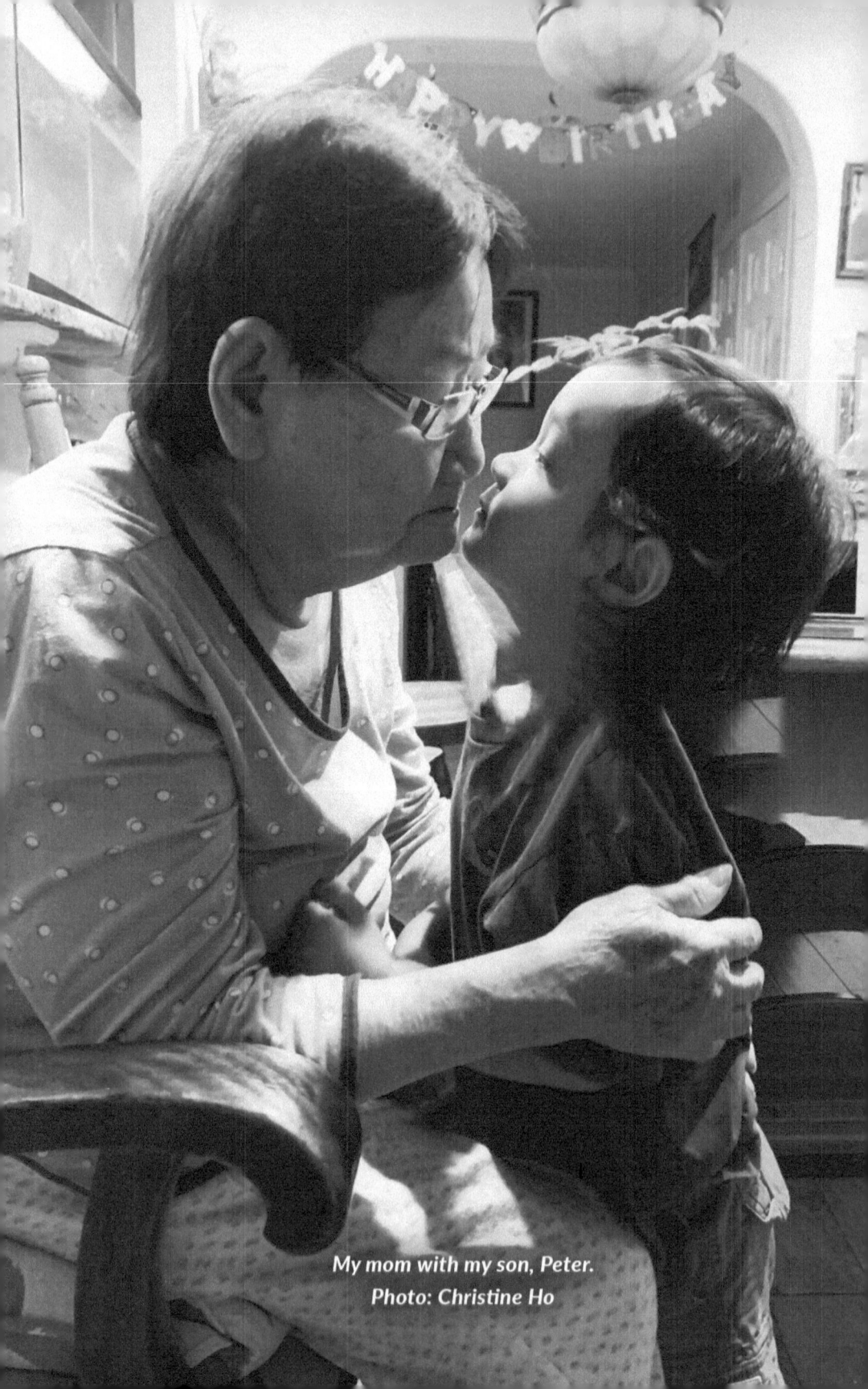

My mom with my son, Peter.
Photo: Christine Ho

Chapter 1

The Day Everything Changed

April 30, 1975

As tears ran down her cheeks, my mother slowly cut her beautiful red nails from her fingers one by one. I was nine years old and could not understand why my mother was crying. Half-naked, as I was most of the time - like the rest of the poor kids in our neighborhood - I sat next to her on a cemented bench that belonged to our neighbors, Mr. and Mrs. Seven.

"Mom, what is wrong? Why are you crying?" I asked innocently. She didn't answer me.

Instead, she shooed me away. "Go out front of the alley and look for your dad." To my understanding, most poor people lived in the alley in Viet Nam, and the rich people lived in the main street. I was unsure why Mom was telling me to look for Dad and why she was so sad. It was the day that changed Viet Nam for better or worse, depending on which side you were on.

Reluctantly, I tried to make my way to the top of the alley to look for my dad, and as I passed from one home to the next,

A Runaway Teenager

I saw people were gathering in small groups. The usual aroma of burning wood for evening meals from the alley was mopped up by the intense conversation palpable with anxiety. Fewer children were playing in the alley. And the cacophony of a densely packed neighborhood had subsided. By then, I could understand that the people in the alley were talking about the war. The war was over, and the communists had won, but the people did not seem to be happy with the news. Perhaps many men in the alley were fighting against the communist party.

Eventually, I made it to the main street to look for my father. The main street was filled with people rushing past each other hurriedly to go home to their family. I could not see my dad among the throng of people, so I sat on an electric pole patiently waiting for Dad. After a few hours, I went back to the alley and headed home to tell my mother that I did not see Dad, although other men in the alley had made it home. When arrived, I saw that Mom had lit a candle because the electricity was out again. Our family could feel the sadness in the air as we sat around Mom while she was sobbing quietly, waiting for Dad to come home. Mom knew that our lives were about to change profoundly under the communist regime.

Dad made it home late that night without a wound or bruise on his body. Before Dad came home, there were rumors that those in the military were subject to beating or torture because they were fighting against the communist party. Dad came home without his military fatigues, and his countenance depicted a sorrow of a man who just lost the war. All eight of us were finally under one roof with Mom and Dad.

My name is Quyen Ha. I saw a movie with an actor named Anthony Quinn, and I liked it because my name sounded like Quinn. It was probably the easiest thing to help people from trying to twist their tongue to pronounce my name. Ha, my last name, was a lot easier to explain. I would tell people just like "Ha-Ha-Ha." I would laugh out loud to show how easy it was to say my last name. Some people would laugh hysterically. After that, it seemed as if all the stereotypes, biases, and negatives associated with an Asian person with a Ha last name vanished. This method worked as an adult, but a Ha last name in high school was an arduous task to defend from kids teasing me. I was born in My Tho City, Viet Nam.

My dad was a Morse code teacher in the military. He rarely came home until the weekends, and that was when we got to go to the movies and get ice cream. My mother was a chief household officer, staying home and taking care of the kids and the household chores. I didn't know how Mom could take care of eight kids cooking, cleaning, and chasing us around to discipline us. I was the sixth child of the family, with four brothers and three sisters.

Before April 30th, 1975, we were - you could say - poor, but we were content because there were many families in our alley that didn't have what we had. We knew this because whenever we had extra food, Mom would always give it to the less fortunate families in the alley. We had three meals a day. We were able to attend school about half a day, five days a week. We slept on the concrete floor with a small sheet made of small bamboo strings. Mom and Dad had a bed that was made of wood. Mom cooked with wood and oil stoves for our meals, and we didn't have a refrigerator or a washer and dryer. Mom washed all our clothes with her hands. Mom toiled all day long to care for us. Mom fed us and clothed us with the money Dad made and worked odd jobs to make ends meet. We were happy and obedient children, and we were loved and disciplined by Mom and Dad. We never complained about not having enough food or toys to play with, although some of the neighborhood kids were much better off than we were.

Our home was located approximately midway of the alley, and it was covered with bricks on four sides, like most of the homes in Viet Nam. The roof, like others in our neighborhood, was covered with metal roof sheets. All the homes were wall to wall against each other, meaning that we could hear the conversations our neighbors were having, and they could listen to ours. Our home faced similar homes in the neighborhood, separated only by a sewage drain. The drain was supposed to be covered up, but the contractor responsible for maintaining it skimmed the money and didn't use quality cement to cover the drain. The neighbors were fed up with the cheating, so they stopped contributing money to fix the problem. They didn't mind that whenever it rained, the sewage would drain into their yard, including ours. To access our home, we had to walk through the drainage that contained sewage and hoped that we didn't catch any bacteria through our feet. Looking back, I am thankful that we never got flesh-eating bacteria from walking in the sewage on our bare feet. We didn't have running water, but we had a toilet drained to a septic tank connected to the main drain in front of the house.

Our home had a front yard; the middle was the living room. The kitchen and bathroom were the last part of the home. We had a second story for another sleeping section. My brothers and I slept on the second story from time to time until it was not safe to sleep because the wood was rotting. We used a mosquito net every night when we went to sleep to protect us from these giant mosquitoes. Whenever I was sleeping with Mom, she would use a small lantern to kill the mosquitoes that invaded our net. They were aggressive and ready to attack us for our blood. My older brothers and sisters slept on the floor, but they didn't have the lantern to catch the mosquitoes, so from time to time, I could hear them slap the mosquitoes with their hands against their bodies. The slapping pattern could be rhythmic when five or six people were doing it simultaneously because there were too many mosquitoes. Whenever the rain came, the floor would get a little cooler, and it was easier to sleep. We loved it when the rain came because we could hear the rain hitting the metal sheet roof. Most of the time, it was soothing and comforting to sleep, but when the rain was heavy during the monsoon season, the sound of the heavy rain hitting the roof was like thousands of bullets were coming down on it. That was when the younger children got to sleep with Mom and Dad.

There were two ways for us to get water. One of the benefits of the rain was that it provided water. When there was no rain, Mom or my older sisters, Heather and Mary, had to buy water from Ms. Nine, who lived in front of the alley. They carried it home with two buckets until we could fill our tank. When Ms. Nine didn't have the water, they had to go about half a mile to get water. They could carry two buckets at a time, each hooked to one end of a thick bamboo stick. When I got older, this task was given to me, but I couldn't carry both buckets on my shoulders, so I carried only one bucket with my hands. The water was too heavy for my little hands, and there was so much sloshing in the bucket that by the time I got to the house, the bucket was only half full. Mom would grunt a little because the water was not cheap, but she was happy that I tried my best to help the family.

For the next few months, Mom and Dad discussed how we were going to live our lives.

"We should sell the house and move the family to the country," Dad yelled at Mom one night. "You know my parents left us some land."

"They hardly left us anything. There isn't room for all of us," Mom replied. "We need to stay in the city for our children's sake."

Their arguments were often loud and made us very sad to hear them. I was hurt from listening to my parents argue and embarrassed because the neighbors could hear them, but we would do whatever they decided.

Dad wanted to sell the house and move all of us to the country where his dad had given him a piece of land after he died. My grandparents had six kids. Like many Vietnamese families, their children were given numbers for names - Two through Seven. I wasn't sure why they were named with numbers, but I surmised that the reason that Vietnamese people called their children with numbers was that they had too many of them, and the easiest way to remember them was to number them. But the number did not start with One. I don't recall hearing anyone with number One as a name. Perhaps this was less intimidating for the rest of the children who were not fortunate enough to be number One children. When my grandparents died, they gave each kid a piece of land. Dad had the smallest piece of land compared to his siblings. Unlike his siblings who stayed home in the countryside, Dad had gone to the city to join the military. I never met my grandparents on Dad's side. When my grandparents died, they were buried on the piece of land given to Uncle Seven, my father's youngest brother. It was commonplace for people in the country to bury their loved ones on their land because there were no burial sites that I could remember. This way, their loved ones could visit them whenever they wished.

Mom wanted us to stay in the city, and she argued that the children knew nothing about living in the country or farming.

They fought for a few months. Eventually, Dad moved to the country without Mom, and we were given an option to go with Dad or stay with Mom. Two of my older brothers, Mark and Nick, and I moved with Dad. We were so excited to move to the country to be with Dad and to play with our cousins. I was excited because I had never been to the country up to that point. Mom had many reasons not to move to the country with Dad. She grew up in the big cities. She knew nothing about living in the country. And she wasn't sure if we could finish school in the country.

Mom's decision to stay in the city was the wisest move she made for all of us, even though she ended up losing her husband. She made an incredible sacrifice for all her children.

Chapter 2

Life with Dad

May 1976

We packed our bags and moved with Dad to his hometown, where he would grow crops to sell as a business. We took a boat from our home in the city to the countryside. The boat ride was about two hours. The boat was large enough to carry around thirty to forty people and lots of cargo, including live animals and produce, to be sold at the market.

When we made it to the country, we had to stay with Dad's brother Uncle Seven, because Dad did not have a home on his land.

The country life differed from the city life. The roads were not cemented, and there was no electricity. When the sun went down, the streets were pitch-black. We couldn't make out each other's faces just a few feet away. People stayed inside unless it was necessary to travel. Coconut leaves made into a bundle were lit as a lamp to guide us to travel after dark. To keep the fire going, we had to swing the bundle back and forth as we walked. There was only one street that allowed people to travel from their home to downtown, and the river was another way to travel to downtown and other towns. Most homes were conveniently located just a few yards from either side of the river, which provided water for cooking and drinking, washing our laundry, and other needs.

Our aunt's and uncle's homes did not have indoor bathrooms, so to use the restroom, there were two choices. Uncle Seven had a pond he used as a toilet because, in this pond, the fish only ate fecal matter. In the middle of the pond, there was a root from a tree that connected the pond from one end to the other, and in the middle of the root, my uncle put up a four-walled structure made of coconut leaves that barely covered your behind when you sat down. People could still see your face when you were in it. We loved to use this toilet because the fish would surface with their tail splashing as they tried to fight for their food. From time to time, we would pretend to use the toilet but only drop dirt in the pond. The fish responded only mildly. I presumed that they could tell which was food. Uncle Seven rarely let us eat the fish, but now and then, he would fish out a few fish and cook them for us. Yes, we ate the fish, and they were good.

Another option for a toilet was on land. We picked up a grub hoe or shovel, grabbed some banana leaves moistened by the morning mist for toilet paper, then looked for a suitable spot to dig a hole that was large enough for the business at hand. The greatest challenge was finding a place that nobody could see you.

We covered the hole up when the business was over. However, the next challenge was not to dig the same hole for subsequent use. It happened often, and we always laughed about it.

After a few weeks of living with my uncle, my dad was taken away to a reeducation camp. The reeducation was used to educate most, if not all, people involved in the fighting against the communist party. Dad never talked about the camp, and I didn't dare to ask him about it. However, when he came home from the camp, he lost his beer belly, and he did not look like the father I knew.

While Dad was in the camp, my brothers and I ended up living with different relatives. When Aunt Five came to visit us at Uncle Seven's home and saw that I was getting along well with her youngest son, she asked me to move in with her - I accepted. Mark and Nick lived with my Uncle Seven. I lived with Aunt Five about a few miles from them, so we didn't get to see each other. Aunt Five was kind enough to have me in her home. She took care of me, just like her youngest son. He and I were like brothers, and we did everything together, including swimming in the river, fishing in the pond, and doing chores that were given to us by his parents. It was summer, so we were always running around having fun, chasing cicadas, grasshoppers, and dragonflies. When the night fell, we chased fireflies. Life was innocent and fun for a few months. I enjoyed living with Aunt Five, but I never saw Mark and Nick, and I missed them. Eventually, I moved in with my cousin Four, Aunt Five's oldest son, and his wife to be closer to my brothers.

A Runaway Teenager

I lived with cousin Four for a few weeks, and I worked with him often on his land. One day we were digging a ditch, and he was trying to tell me to do something. I didn't understand. Coming from the city, there were many things I didn't know how to do on the farm. Cousin Four got upset and scolded me for not understanding him. I apologized to him and asked him to show me how to do it. I didn't appreciate the scolding, but when he used derogative remarks about my mother, I decided it was time for me to find another place to live because that was verboten. Even as a ten-year-old boy, I didn't appreciate people calling my mother names. I knew he was angry with me when he said it, but I still had to run away from these bad people, as I defined them. So I asked my Uncle Four, my father's older brother, to stay with him. His home was even closer to Uncle Seven's home. I was getting closer and closer to my brothers.

Living in Uncle Four's home was a lot more fun compared to the last two homes. He had seven kids, but when I lived with him, there were only four kids in the home. My cousins Five, Seven, and Eight were the boys, and cousin Six was the girl. I learned how to climb coconut trees, peel a coconut, paddle a boat, cook with wood, and anything that would help me survive the country life. We went to bed around eight o'clock in the evening and woke up when the rooster made its first crow for the morning, which was around five o'clock. That was their alarm. As usual, cousin Six was up and had breakfast ready for the boys to work in the rice field. I didn't know about hard work until my cousins showed me how to plant rice stalks. After our breakfast was done, we walked to the field as the sun slowly came up from the horizon to show that it would be a hot day. Along the way, we could see the mist on the banana leaves on the trees that were collected from the night before, and as we accidentally hit the tree with our tools, we could hear the water from the leaves hitting the ground softly to remind us they were still alive. The smell of the morning in the country was pure and inviting at the same time. The only thing that would disturb such purity was smoke from a neighbor's wood-cooking stove.

After a short distance, we made it to the rice fields. We divided up the stalks for each quadrant of the fields and were ready to go to work. As I bent over to grab each stalk to plant it in the ground, I didn't know that my back was going to be parallel to the ground to plant for the entire field. The next stalk had to be about a few inches apart from the last stalk and straight across the area. We did that until all our fields were full of rice stalks. I only lasted for about one and a half days. My cousins were a few years older than I was, but they were muscular. They did this every year and never complained about how hard life was. I looked up to them as I learned about the hardships of country life.

After our work was done, we played together. By now, I could play with my brother Nick and our cousins as often as I liked. Mark was hanging out with older cousins. Swimming in the river was our favorite and cheapest thing to do. Along the riverbank, there were trees with giant branches that swung out to the water, and that was our diving board. The sun was in our faces, cicadas were singing our summer music, and we swam with no worries, for tomorrow was another fun day awaiting us. We only stopped swimming to drink water and forage for food. If we were to have yuca or sweet potatoes, that was a great day for us, and when that luxury was not available, we would search for baby corn on my dad's land. Every time we went to look for corn on my dad's land, we found it, and we ate it raw. It felt like a miracle that the corn was always there for me.

Artist: Sudipta Steve Dasgupta

A Runaway Teenager

Soccer was our next favorite pastime because we had enough kids to make two teams. We used dried-up coconuts as our balls. We didn't have money for a soccer ball that was made of plastic. The coconut had a very odd shape, and it was painful on our bare feet. We didn't have shoes to wear, just sandals. In the country, most people didn't wear sandals because it would be laborious to walk on a muddy road, and falling was very common. But for us, coconut soccer balls were a great pleasure, and they were always available because dry coconuts were ubiquitous on both sides of the road, in the homes, and the ditches.

Watching crickets fight each other was another summer activity for us. However, we didn't have money to purchase and care for the crickets, so we made friends with the kids who did, and watched their crickets fight. When the sun was out and dinner and evening chores were done, we would listen to a book reading program on the radio, mostly novels, and my cousins enjoyed it every night until they finished the complete story, which could take months. Uncle Four was fortunate enough to have a radio at his home, but I didn't live with him long enough for the complete novel.

While I was living with Uncle Four, his wife came home after an extended business trip. I was in the front yard when she came in. I had never met her, but I was worried that she might not like me being in her home when she wasn't there. My cousins gossiped that she was more strict and hard to deal with than my uncle - the rumor wasn't true. So I left Uncle Four's home that afternoon without meeting her. I went down to the river and watched the tide go in and out. I could have gone to Uncle Seven's home, where Nick was, but I didn't want them to have to feed another mouth, although they would have taken me in without hesitation. While I was down the river, I was thinking about my father and hoping he was home so we could be together. I had moved enough from one home to the next, and nothing was working for me. When the evening came, I moved away from the river and found a bench underneath a fruit tree that had fruit about to fall any day now.

Artist: Sudipta Steve Dasgupta

As darkness took over, the familiar sound of frogs and other creatures surrounded me. The waves were lapping against the riverbanks not too far from where I was. I lay quietly and prayed that Dad would come home. But my hunger pang quickly overwhelmed my fear and loneliness, and I hoped that the fruit would drop soon. I waited a long while, but the fruit never came. I rolled to my side as tears came down my cheeks. I shut my eyes and let the hunger pang invade my dream into the night.

The warmth of the cemented bench woke me from the longest night of my life. What happened to the fruit was the only thing on my mind this morning. I slowly opened my eyes and looked up at the tree, and to my happiness, the fruit no longer hung on to the tree. I knew then that it had to be on the ground. It was a disappointment because the fruit had shattered into pieces on the ground, but this morning, nothing was stopping me from my breakfast and maybe my only meal for the day. When I finished, there was no trace of that fruit in the cracks or crevices on the ground to convince anyone that any fruit had fallen.

For the time being, the river was the only friend I had, and I didn't think about where I would go tomorrow or the day after. When my hunger pang came back, I was forced to leave the river and look for food. The only place that seemed to be a miracle for me was my dad's land, where we found a patch of land with corn. Amazingly, I found some baby corn to get me through the day, and I was back to the river and the bench ready for another night. The following day my cousins and Nick found me, and they were wondering where I was the last few days. I didn't tell them the truth. Nick told me to come live with Uncle Seven, so I did.

Dad came home after the communist regime reeducated him. It took Dad and our uncles a few weeks to build our home on his land. The frame was made with large and small bamboo trees, and the coconut leaves made the sides and the roof. The roof was low enough that the chickens and snakes could live on it. These animals would slide off the roof whenever the rain came. It was not raining cats and dogs, but raining chickens and snakes. There was a clay stove to cook with wood in the back of the house and a round barrel next to the house to store water from the river or the rain. The bamboo bed was bumpy and rockier than the bench by the river. However small or primitive the house was, I was content and joyful because we had our own home.

Our life began in the little house that Dad built with his brothers. Besides being a Morse code teacher, Dad also knew how to cut hair. Dad could grow three crops on his land depending on the season, including watermelons, string beans, and sugarcanes. Every morning before Dad left the house, our chores were taught to us and expected to get done by the time Dad got home. Our usual routine was to water the crops in the morning with Dad. Dad then went to work to cut hair for people by riding his bike all around the neighborhood, far and near. The water for the crops was from the river in front of our home. With a small bucket one by one, Nick and I watered our crops on about one acre of land. Mark usually had bigger jobs to do because he was six years older than I was and stronger. Trimming the leaves of the sugarcanes was the next painful chore because the leaves were razor sharp, and there was no way we could avoid cutting our hands. At the end of each season, our city boys' hands were no longer recognizable. To feed the hogs and chickens, a banana tree needed to be chopped in small chunks then stored for later use. Preparing for dinner was our last chore for the day. Dad told us what to cook for dinner before going to work. On a lucky day, we would have fish or pigeon, which needed to be purchased. Dad taught us how to kill the pigeon, remove the feathers, and marinate it. Nick was the head chef, and I was the sous chef.

By the time Dad got home, we had set the small table in the front of the home for dinner. Sometimes, we waited a long while before Dad got home because he had to travel farther out to get business. Dad would ring his bell on his bicycle to alert us when he was at the front of the home. Under the flickering light of the lantern, we ate dinner together joyously as we recapitulated the chores we had done for the day. Most of the time, Dad was happy with our work. However, the final decision was when Dad inspected our work the next day, and if it was not to his satisfaction, we did the same chores again. On school nights, after we finished our dishes, Nick and I did our homework then went to bed. Mark wasn't in school at that time. In return for a bedtime story, we massaged Dad's back and legs. Dad eventually ran out of stories, but we still gave him a massage every night.

The river remained my secret friend for the time I was with Dad. I immersed my childhood in this river from the very first time that I moved to the country. I felt happy when the river was high, so high that it could almost reach the edge of the house, and sad when the river was low, so low that I could walk on it from one side to the other. This river was not only the source of my emotional support but the source of life for all the people in Vietnam.

Chapter 3

Back with Mom in the City

September 1977

After living with Dad for a little more than a year, I realized that country life was not for me. I missed Mom and the rest of my brothers and sisters in the city. Mark also wanted to go back to the city to live with Mom. One afternoon while Dad was at work, Mark and I caught the last boat for the city. When the boat was pushed off from the riverbank, I looked back at Nick one last time, hoping Nick would change his mind and go with us. He sadly waved at me, and I waved back. We weren't sure when we would see each other again.

As the boat moved away from the bank of the river, all the memories from swimming in the river, chasing cicadas, playing soccer with coconuts, and messing with poop-eating fish rushed back to me. I wanted to jump into the river and swim back to Nick, who was still looking at me. I turned away and hid my tears because I didn't want Nick to feel sad. The boat slowly moved north, and soon, I was able to see the old bench that I had slept on and the fruit tree that gave me an excellent breakfast not too long ago. Quietly, I said goodbye to the river, the bench,

A Runaway Teenager

and the fruit tree as the boat picked up speed away from them. I knew Dad would be upset when he came home because he wouldn't approve of our leaving, but my living in the country had come to an end, and my habit of running away continued.

As the boat got closer to the city, the river got wider and busier, and the lights were brighter because there was electricity. After a two-hour ride, the boat finally docked. We stepped off the boat into familiar sights and sounds of city life. People were moving at a rapid pace. Food vendors were inviting customers to buy their food by singing out short phrases about their products. At every block, a cigarette vendor was sitting quietly with his or her little cabinet displaying each label of cigarettes through the glass window with a small lantern on top of the cabinet to be a lighter for people who didn't have a match. The smell from the food vendors was making me hungry as I tried to walk past them. A three-wheeled carriage was a simple way of travel for people to get around the city; however, tonight, for a couple of runaway kids, that was a luxury we couldn't afford. The thought of getting off a three-wheeled carriage in front of the alley while the half-naked kids from the alley looked on with envy imbued my heart with joy. My thought was interrupted by the smell of urine, diesel exhaust, and cigarette smoke, which could be nauseating yet affirmed the reality of the city life waiting for me.

My old neighborhood was within my view as I quickened my footsteps. And there it was, open sewage, half-naked and barefoot kids chasing each other. The usual banter of the evening as people went about their business welcomed me back to city life. Mom was surprised and worried when she saw Mark and me unhook the front gate and step into our yard because Nick usually came with me to the city to visit. Over the next few hours, Mom asked me what made me come back to town. She immediately enrolled me in school for fourth grade.

Life in the city with Mom was very different from country life. Electricity was more available most days of the week, although from time to time we would be without it for a few days. Mom was still cooking food with wood. The kids in my neighborhood were cunning and creative at the same time. Living in the city, we could always hook up with one of the rich kids for a plastic soccer ball. Our days of playing soccer with coconuts were a memory. Coconuts weren't readily available in the city.

Bowling was a one-pin game. The pin was an aluminum can whenever we could find one. We set the pin in the middle of a chalk-drawn square on the ground. Each player took turns knocking down the pin with his shoe or a stick if he didn't have shoes. The rich kids usually played for money, and the poor kids just played for fun. Marbles was a more challenging game, but we loved it. This game required an ability to aim and a flexible middle finger to hit your opponent's marbles with your marble. Some kids could even hit their targets from five feet away. The city kids were more aggressive with their fighting crickets because they were trained to fight for money. I played with the neighbor's kids whenever school was out.

Most afternoons, we also teamed up and went to the river to swim. This part of the river was a dumping site for many people who lived nearby. Nothing was going to stop us from our daily swim in the river. At one time, I could swim across the river by myself without help from the inner tube.

Music was another form of entertainment for us. It seemed as if there was always a guitar to mess with when the sun went down, and on a moonlit night, we could play late into the night, singing our favorite songs. For a bunch of kids without a formal musical education, we did our best to entertain ourselves and enjoyed it to the fullest.

By the time I made it to sixth grade, the economy had taken a nosedive, and our lives were in turmoil. Mom was the only breadwinner in the family with seven kids to feed. She did all she could to provide for us, but going to bed without a meal was more frequent in our family. The communist economy wasn't working well for the country. Jobs were scarce, there wasn't enough rice to feed the people, and food prices skyrocketed. This economic system was hitting the poor the hardest. One year when rice was scarce, we had to buy this grain from the government, and the origin of the grain was unknown. Every time we ate it, we developed pus-filled lesions all over our bodies. My oldest sister was always there to look out for us whenever she could. She worked at a daycare center, so after the kids ate their lunch that their parents packed for them, she took the leftover food and brought it home for us.

We survived on that until my sister lost her job. Sometimes, I visited my neighbors around lunchtime, pretending to borrow something but hoping they would be kind enough to offer me some food. It didn't matter how skillful I was; eventually, the neighbors caught on to my schemes. Mom was unaware, but I didn't think she would object when she had seven kids, and one of them could find a way to feed himself.

Tough times continued to wreak havoc in our neighborhood. By the time I got to seventh grade, I had one pair of pants and one shirt for school. Immediately after class, I rushed home and washed my pants and shirt with my hands to prepare them for the next day. When the clothes were hung on the clotheslines, I prayed for no rain and that thieves wouldn't steal my clothes. People were stealing anything to sell for food. Having to wear the same clothes to school every day was an embarrassment for me. The girls were gossiping about me, the one-pants-one-shirt guy.

When the situation was unbearable, skipping classes was my only choice. It was almost a thrill and an adventure to jump out of the classroom window while the teacher wasn't paying attention. The rendezvous was at a tamarind tree outside the school for those who were able to jump out the window. We shared a cigarette, if there was one, and talked until it was time to walk home. At first, I only skipped the last hour of the day, but eventually, I cut the entire day. Our group also accumulated more kids by the end of the semester. We were considered the dust of life. Mom didn't know about my school activities.

A Runaway Teenager

As the economy continued to spiral out of control, the communist government also flexed its muscles to control its people. All books, music, and literature that were associated with the previous regime were searched and destroyed. Young men weren't allowed to have long hair or bell-bottom pants. Every intersection had cops pulling people over for having long hair or bell-bottom pants or any garment that was deemed unsuitable to the communist regime. In some cases, the hair and the pants were cut on sight. Every member in a home had to register with the local police and ask permission to travel out of town. Houses could be searched at any given time without probable cause. Curfew was imposed daily. People who had relatives associated with the previous government couldn't apply for jobs with the communist regime.

Speaking against the communist regime was proscribed, and those who were brave enough even to whisper a scintilla of disagreement were sent to the reeducation camp. Young men turning eighteen were drafted automatically to fight for the regime. The wealthy had their fortunes removed from their homes. We witnessed our freedoms and livelihoods being usurped by the very government that was supposed to be for the people, not taken from the people. For the South Vietnamese people, the Draconian law was their fear, but to live it was atrocious. These rules started as soon as the communist party took over the country, but they became a part of our lives when the communist party had complete control of its citizens a few years later.

By land or by sea, young or old, people were looking for a way to escape for their freedom. I had read some of the letters from the people in our neighborhood who had made it out of Viet Nam. People in the neighborhood would tell stories about those who made it - and those who didn't. One year the government even allowed people to escape, but they had to pay. We knew about this program, but we didn't have the money for it. This program was soon stopped because there were too many people leaving the country.

Children escaping without parents and parents escaping without children were not unusual events. They gave up their homes and fortunes to pay human traffickers to walk them to Cambodia or Laos. This journey was dangerous and was not a guarantee. People often lost their lives or ended up in prison, and when they came out of prison, they became destitute and homeless. We knew some of these people. The most common way to escape was by boat. The going price was about two ounces of gold per person. Finding a boat for the journey was harrowing and risky because if anyone was suspected of attempting to escape, they immediately went to prison. Escaping by boat was perilous and gruesome because of the unforgiving tempestuous sea. Those who made it past Viet Nam's border often got lost and perished without a trace. One of my childhood friends was never found after his escape. Some ran out of food and water. Urine was their source of hydration, and dead people were their food. Some were captured by the pirates. The women were raped, and the men were tortured and killed. These stories were sent back from the witnesses who were lucky enough to survive the ordeal.

Our family endured the suffering under the government's watchful eye; however, we knew that this was not the life that God had given us. Even though the risk of being captured or killed was irrefutable, we were willing to give up our lives for our freedom. In our home, my oldest brother, Tri (pronounced like "tree"), made his first attempt when he was seventeen years old. Tri was caught and sent to hard labor prison for a few years. In this prison, he was required to work from sunup to sundown. There was not enough food to survive, so Mom had to bring food to him monthly. Tri managed to survive his imprisonment and made it home. He hardly talked about his life in prison, but we knew it was punishing for him.

Tri was a talented and caring person. He taught himself how to play the guitar. We didn't have a piano at home, so Tri usually took me to church early so he could learn how to play the piano and the organ. He played it so well that the church invited him to play for the choir. Tri helped Mom care for us seven days a week, and he never complained. Tri also volunteered to teach illiterate adults how to read and write a few nights a week. We were about eight years apart, so we didn't hang out much when we were in Viet Nam, but he was my disciplinarian. Although Tri never had to discipline me physically, when he spoke to me, I would obey. I respected Tri and looked up to him because he was the oldest brother in the family, and he worked hard to help Mom care for us. Tri was always looking out for me. Occasionally, when Tri saw that I was hanging out with the kids in the neighborhood and we were behaving mischievously, he would pull me out of the group and take me to church with him. I never complained when we went to church together. Sometimes, I sat outside after church to wait for Tri to finish practicing the organ or the piano and walk home together. I felt very comfortable being with Tri. The neighborhood kids respected and loved him because he taught them all, including me, how to play the guitar. Tri was my role model.

While Tri was away, life was transforming for me in so many ways. I decided that school could not provide me with a good future in Viet Nam, especially with one pair of pants and one shirt. Mother disapproved of my actions, but she knew the best choice for me and us was freedom. At thirteen years old, I started smoking cigarettes and drinking alcohol with people who could provide it.

On one occasion, I lay on the street not too far from the house after imbibing a large rice liquor with a friend. I was yelling and cursing at people who were enjoying watching a drunken teenager. The crowd grew larger and larger until word got to Mom that her son was embarrassing himself a few blocks from her home. Mom came and picked me up and took me home. During my ride home, my level of inebriation was getting deeper. I thought I heard Mom say, "Your butt is in trouble in the morning." That behavior never happened again. My

A Runaway Teenager

misbehaving was reprehensible, but Mom knew I was always there for her. I helped Mom with her business as much as possible, but I was praying for an opportunity to escape.

Chapter 4

Attempted Escape

May 1979

Prison didn't deter Tri from escaping Viet Nam. If anything, it motivated him because freedom was his ultimate goal. Once Tri was released from prison, he was determined to try again. Although our family lived an impecunious life, Mom negotiated with the boat owner to take Tri and me. Our uncle could pay for our next escape if we made it to America, and it was critically important for us to keep our planning a secret.

A few months after waiting patiently, a man came to our home and picked us up and took us to another city. In general, people would find a fisherman who had been fishing in the ocean near the border and was willing to escape. Once this relationship was established, the middleman would recruit people like us to take care of expenses. The planning and recruiting had to be done clandestinely.

We said goodbye to Mom. She wasn't sure if we could escape successfully because of Tri's previous attempt.

A Runaway Teenager

"Mom, I think he is here to pick us up for the trip," I said quietly when the middleman came through our front doors.

"Well, what are you waiting for?" Mom responded nervously. "Pack up your things and go."

As we walked out of the house, Mom was still standing there, watching us, knowing that she might not see us again. We were put on a small fishing boat along with seventy or eighty other people. People were everywhere. Tri and I were on the upper deck. I sat next to the edge of the boat and could touch the water in the river. I was running away from home one more time.

Our boat departed from the shoreline as the darkness blanketed the sky. There wasn't a sound to be heard from the people on the boat except the sputtering of the boat engine pushing us toward the border. I was excited and nervous at the same time. All I could think was by morning we would be in the open sea. Freedom awaited us. It was the moment Tri and I waited for, a chance to embrace freedom.

The excitement in my head was quickly interrupted by multiple gunshots. Those were no firecrackers. Living in a war-torn country, the sound of gunshots was very discernible to us. In elementary school, sometimes the bombing was so close, it shook the building. We would hide under our desks, and when the bombing stopped, we went right back to learning our ABCs. There were times I could hear the bombing in the distance while walking to school. I was scared, but I never turned around because of a little bombing here and there. Mom and Dad were concerned because there was an elementary school accidentally bombed and a lot of children died, but they always insisted that we get an education. So bombing or no bombing, there was no recess in our home.

Pandemonium broke out when gunshots were heard from our boat. The coast guards were yelling and screaming for us to stop the boat. The people and the children were crying, not knowing what just happened. I knew what happened. Tri came up to me and said that we had been caught. I couldn't see his face, but in his voice, I heard the anxiety and fear of what would happen to him if he was captured again. A few minutes after the gunshot rang out, our boat was pulled next to the guards' boat, and the guards came on our boat with AK-47s pointing in our faces. It was the reality now that the Vietnamese coast guards had captured us. Our boat was forced to follow the guards' boat to the prison.

My dreams of being freed were pulverized, and I wasn't sure what would happen to us next. I sat silently watching the guards and wondered how they could capture us so quickly. It took almost a day to get our boat closer to the prison.

"Little brother," Tri whispered, "if you can slip off the boat, swim for the banks of the river and go home so you can tell Mom what happened." Tri knew I could swim the river because of my mischievous days swimming the river without Mom's approval. I wanted to and wasn't afraid of the river, but the guards were ready to entertain any escapee with their AK-47s.

The rain had stopped a few minutes before we docked. The guards put us on a bus to be taken to the prison. We weren't allowed to talk during the bus ride. A few hours later, the bus stopped, and they let us out to use a tree or bush as a restroom. I walked away from the bus while the guards were looking the other way. I hid behind a tree, pretending I was using the bathroom while hoping they didn't see me when it was time to leave. It was my second opportunity to get away from imprisonment. Although the escape in the river would have been easier, now was my only chance.

Suddenly, I heard the guard call out for all of us to get on the bus. I stood still and did not move an inch. They didn't check us for IDs or write our names when they captured us, so if I were to stay back, there was no way they could tell who was missing. A few minutes later, a guard was making his last roundup. I could hear his footsteps getting closer and closer to the tree where I was hiding. My heart was racing so fast. I knew I could slide around the tree just as he was about to see me and slide back when he came back around. The guard stopped a few steps from the tree and took a deep drag of his cigarette, and I could hear the clanking of his AK-47. He threw his cigarette to the ground and took the steps past the tree and me. The thought of being shot in the back with an AK-47 froze me from moving around the tree. The guard turned around and saw me behind the tree. "Get back to the bus!"

Artist: Sudipta Steve Dasgupta

We made it to the prison around midnight. The prison was dark because there was no electricity, and by this time, the prisoners were sleeping, so there was no welcoming for the new guys. Tri was sent to a different hut because he was older. They threw me in a hut with a roof made of coconut leaves and a bed made of bamboo, just like the one I used to sleep in when I lived with Dad in the country. They gave me a bowl of rice. I didn't know what else was in it. I took a handful, put it in my mouth, and spat it out quickly because it was all salt. That was my first taste of prison food.

In the darkness of this prison, I found a spot on the bamboo bed and lay down with my eyes wide open. I was scared and alone, a political prisoner at thirteen years old. How long would I be in here? Did Mom know that we were captured? It was going to be an embarrassment when I made it home to face the kids in the neighborhood. The people who got caught and made it home were often ridiculed for their unsuccessful escape. If they made it, they were just lucky. If they were never heard from again, they were just victims of the sea. The night took over all those thoughts as I slipped into my dreams of the ocean and the dolphins.

The morning came with the noise from the prison guards to wake up all the new inmates. We were gathered in the prison's courtyard. I was so happy to see Tri, and he told me to lie about my age to get out of prison sooner. Tri told me he would try to lie about his age, but his mustache was growing by the minute, so he was not sure if he could get away with it. Our personal information was taken one by one in the courtyard. All valuables were confiscated. While we were waiting in the yard, I saw the middleman who hooked us up with the boat owner being whisked away in a military jeep. I didn't think anything of it until I was out of prison, but this was a setup between him and the coast guards to make money. He knew that if we had made it out to the ocean, we all would have been dead. There were too many of us on that little boat. I was released from prison after two weeks because of my age. I survived prison with whatever food they gave me and mooched off the wealthy inmates whose families brought them food weekly. Tri was transferred to a hard labor prison. I only saw Tri once in the courtyard.

Walking rapidly through my old neighborhood with my crestfallen head, attempting to avoid the neighborhood kids, I was stopped when the kids accosted me and asked why I had not been seen in the last few weeks. They knew the answer but just wanted to rough me up a little. I told them the truth and hurried home to see Mom. Mom was not surprised when she saw me. She knew we were captured because of the rumors from members of the families who were on the boat. Mom was saddened by Tri, whom she knew would be in prison for a long time. I told Mom the whole story about the trip and the middleman. She agreed it was a setup and was very upset about it. Mom didn't know where Tri was transferred to until a few months later when she visited him at the old prison. By now, I was the oldest boy at home, and my desire to leave Viet Nam was unstoppable.

Chapter 5

The Escape

April 1980

The second time Tri was in prison, he met up with Mr. Six, who was also a political prisoner for attempting to escape Viet Nam. Mr. Six took Tri under his wings because Tri was alone, and he was one of the youngest prisoners whose political views impressed him, so he promised to hook up with Tri for another escape when he was released. Mr. Six came to our home from Sai Gon after he made it out of prison to look for Tri. He was disappointed and saddened to know that Tri was still in prison. However, there was a plan for a new escape, and he wanted to see if we could help him recruit people for the trip.

After Mom scraped up all the money she had for our last trip, we had no money to even entertain going with Mr. Six. I asked Mr. Six if I recruited some people, could I go for free? He agreed. He knew that it would be less suspicious for a young person to travel and talk to people than for an adult to do it. I was excited and ready to do my part for this trip. Mom agreed with the deal because she knew this was the best chance for me to escape.

A Runaway Teenager

When I was in school, there was a rumor that my physics teacher had attempted to escape a few times, but he didn't make it. I started with him to see if he was willing to give it another try. We met in a coffee shop where he was working part-time. He paid for the coffee and the cigarettes. At thirteen, I was making a deal for my future.

"Teacher, if there is an opportunity to escape, are you interested?" I asked bluntly after I took a long drag on my cigarette. I wasn't sure if he would kick me out of the coffee shop or call the cops to arrest me.

"Why are you asking me? Have you done this before?" he whispered nervously to make sure that no one was listening.

"I was arrested on my first attempt," I replied.

His skeptical smile vanished. We sat there for a while before he uttered, "Sure. But I must meet with your people to confirm." He added, "I may be able to bring another person."

I was beyond excited because there were two potential escapees to help me with this trip. I arranged for my teacher and his friend to meet Mr. Six to confirm the plans for the trip.

They never told me how much they were paying Mr. Six, and I didn't even want to know. My job was to find people for Mr. Six, and I would get a free ticket. Now and then, while I was still trying to recruit more people, I would meet up with

Mr. Six at his home to update him on what I was doing and help him do whatever needed to be done for the trip. On one occasion, he sent me to meet a boat owner in this little fishing town. After meeting the owner, he was arrested because the cops were suspicious of the new kid in his home. I left his home and reported the event to Mr. Six. We didn't get that boat for the trip. Eventually, Mr. Six was able to negotiate with a different boat owner to plan for the escape.

Tri came home from prison while I was working with Mr. Six. He was supportive of my decision to work for Mr. Six, but he wasn't sure if any of it would come to fruition. Tri also knew Mom had no money to pay for his trip with Mr. Six if he wanted to come.

The waiting game began, and I didn't know anything about the trip because I was not a paid escapee. One night Mom came home from her trip to Sai Gon, where Mr. Six lived. She rushed into the house and started packing my bag with my birth certificate and some clothes. She was talking fast and moving around the house to find things for my trip.

"You've got to travel to Mr. Six's home tonight. I was in Sai Gon, and I visited his home because I hadn't heard from him in a long time. Lots of people were gathering in his home. It looked like they were getting ready for the trip." I didn't know what to say and was saddened by the news. Mom's suspicions were correct because Mr. Six and his group were about to escape without me.

A Runaway Teenager

It was late in the evening when I said goodbye to Mom. I walked to the bus station for the last bus to Sai Gon to see if I could join Mr. Six. We weren't sure if this was the last trip for me, and we weren't sure if Mr. Six still wanted me for his journey. As the bus rolled along the highway, passing each light pole, I felt betrayed if Mr. Six didn't honor our agreement. The feeling of being left behind reminded me that I could trust no one in this business.

The bus stopped halfway before it made it to Sai Gon, and the bus driver informed us that there was a curfew in Sai Gon, so we had to find another way to make it to our final destination. The word panic couldn't even describe how I felt after I heard the news, but I had to focus on a solution.

"Sir, I want to tell you the truth about me going to Sai Gon," I said to the bus driver.

"What is going on, kid?" he asked, taking a long drag of his cigarette.

"Well, I am trying to escape out of Viet Nam," I quivered.

"How old are you, kid? Are you by yourself?" he asked with a stern look.

"I am thirteen, and I am going by myself," I replied.

"Did your parents approve of this escape?" He became even more intense as he threw on the ground what was left of his cigarette.

"Yes, sir," I muttered.

"Okay, kid. The cargo buses can still go through Sai Gon. I know a cargo bus driver that can help you." I watched him talk to a cargo bus driver not too far from his vehicle. After a few minutes, the cargo bus driver waved me down to his bus. He put me in the back of the cabin and told me to stay down because he wasn't supposed to have passengers.

At the first checkpoint, when the guard asked the driver for his identification, everything was copacetic - we were good to go. The second checkpoint was the same. However, at the third checkpoint, when the guard asked the driver to step outside of the truck, I was fearful that he would search inside the cabin or the truck driver would turn me in.

"What are you carrying in your truck?" I heard the guard ask firmly.

"Just vegetables, sir," the truck driver answered politely.

"Are there any other people in the truck beside your helper?" Up until this point, the truck driver was very supportive of me. But this guard was confronting him about additional passengers. The truck driver could be in a lot of trouble if the guard found me in the cabin. Lying flat on the floor, I inched closer to the door, hoping to hear the answer from the truck driver.

"No, officer," he replied calmly.

A Runaway Teenager

"I still have to check your cabin, all right?" the guard demanded. This wasn't what I wanted to hear. I looked frantically around the cabin to find any hole that I could crawl in to hide myself. There was none. All I could do was roll up as close as I could behind the back of the driver's seat, hoping the angle of the seat would give me some cover. As I closed my eyes to pray for God's protection, I could hear the guard's footsteps moving closer to the door. Suddenly, the door flung open. I stopped breathing when I saw the light from the flashlight in the back cabin a few inches away from my face. The guard attempted to lift the back of the seat to have a better view of the floor. When he couldn't remove it the first try, he started to yank on it violently and continually. I could feel the pounding right above my head. Frustrated, the guard stopped. He stepped off the truck and said some curse words to the driver.

I heard the door open again. The guard must have gotten some tools to lift the seat - I was frightened with the thought - but a soft voice said, "We are good to go, kid." I wasn't sure if we were safe until I felt the truck move past the checkpoint.

We made it to Sai Gon by midnight. I walked a few blocks to Mr. Six's home, but it was dark, and I didn't dare knock on the door. I slept sitting up in front of his home just in case he was leaving without me. The following day Mr. Six was upset when he found me in front of his house. I told him why I was there, but he sent me home and told me when the trip was ready, he would come for me. I couldn't know if they took off after I left.

I was devastated because I knew Mr. Six was mendacious to me, but I did my part, and I prayed that God would change Mr. Six's heart and treat me fairly.

Two months after I left Mr. Six's home, his son came to my home one morning to pick me up for the trip. I was shocked but happy. I grabbed my bag and barely said goodbye to Mom and my siblings again. We weren't sure if I could make it this time.

We took a ferry from my home to a small town near the ocean and met up with the rest of the people in a small house. Here, I found out I was the only one that had not been in this home previously. I knew then that Mr. Six had tried a few times without me. After two nights of waiting, it was time for us to get into a small boat then team up with the big boat for our escape. When nighttime came, we were told to walk in silence down to the river because the cops were watching. I could only hear the susurrus of crackling leaves in the trees as we walked silently towards freedom. Within a short distance from the home, we made it to a small boat. The boat slowly departed to the open river, shuttling us to the fishing boat for the escape. It took a few hours for us to meet up with the fishing boat; one by one, we jumped on it. When it was my time to jump, I almost fell off the boat because I missed the handrails. I was so happy when I caught the handrails with my other arm.

The boat was small for forty-two people. We were packed like sardines in the lower deck, and fortunately, the hatch was open when we took off. The main cabin was reserved for the boat owner and his family. The boat inched its way to the border, and nothing could be heard except the engine. I didn't dream of the open sea or freedom this time, but I prayed to God to help us pass the border without hearing an AK-47. The anxiety and fear of getting caught again were unfathomable, yet the thought of getting killed by the ocean didn't scare me.

The minutes went by. Five minutes…ten minutes…thirty minutes. After two hours, I still didn't hear gunshots or screaming from the coast guard. Was it possible that we passed the border? I started to believe it, but I thought to give it a few more hours. My eyes were closed even before I had the chance to count the hours.

The morning sun and the smell of the ocean welcomed me, and I immediately knew that we had made it past the border when I woke that morning. Some boats made it past the border for a few days and still ended up back in Viet Nam because of the inability to navigate the sea. I ignored the negative thought and leaped to the upper deck to see if we were indeed in the ocean. The Viet Nam shorelines were no longer visible with the naked eyes, and there were no other boats within the observing distance.

The vast deep blue sea was beautiful, and I wondered innocently if it was blue. To my surprise, after I scooped up some water in my hand from the ocean, it was not blue. Perhaps, I just wanted to feel the sea for the first time in my life and to appreciate it because it would be the vessel to my freedom. For a moment, I wish Tri had come with me, and we both could have stayed on the upper deck to bask in the sun and the smell of the ocean and watch the dolphins chasing our boat. I couldn't blame Tri for not wanting to try again because five years of hard labor imprisonment could demoralize anyone from attempting to escape; that was the whole idea of imprisonment in Viet Nam. Because of Tri's imprisonment and friendship with Mr. Six, I was able to make this escape. What a high price to pay for his younger brother's freedom. The upper deck was my five-star hotel for the night. It was a thousand-star hotel because I could see a plethora of stars in the sky without the impurity from the city lights.

Our boat pushed farther away from Viet Nam the next three days. On the afternoon of the third day, the captain told us to start praying because we were lost. Each person was allowed to drink one cap of the ten-gallon container three times per day. Although the water was limited, we were more concerned about being lost than being thirsty.

The stories of people being lost at sea who ended up eating each other to survive gave me a disturbing feeling. Drinking my urine to stay alive was comprehensible, but eating my fellow passengers was inconceivable. But I had never faced such a predicament. After the devastating news, I found my favorite spot on the upper deck when the sun was about to set on the horizon, praying to God to save us. I promised God I would live for the rest of my life with love - no more messing with old people, no more bullying other children, and no more stealing communion wine and bread.

We continued to drive our boat in the Pacific Ocean without a known destination for one more day, and on the afternoon of the fifth day, while I was watching the sunset, the people in the main cabin could be seen pointing their fingers toward the sunset. I didn't understand what they were seeing. A few minutes later, more people gathered on the upper deck to point out to me they saw land or an object - I could see nothing except water. Our boat continued to move toward what was supposed to be land, and I wondered if God had heard my prayers.

As our boat got closer and closer, we could see lights. When the darkness took over the night, the lights got brighter, the object became more visible, and we finally realized that it was an oil rig. The supply boat for the oil rig took off as we got closer. Immediately, we raised a banner that said SOS (Save Our Ship) and chased after the supply boat. The captain explained to us later that he went after the supply boat because it could pick us up and take us to a refugee camp - at least he hoped that it would. It was a short chase when the supply boat saw our SOS sign. It stopped and threw us the rope to pull us next to it. I knew our boat was small, but when it was next to the supply boat, our boat was minuscule.

After an unintelligible exchange between the captain of the supply boat and our supposed "translator," we were given water and food and a direction to the nearest refugee camp. As our boat was pushed off from the supply boat, I went up to the highest point in front of the boat - like in *Titanic* but with no Rose - after I was given a piece of white sliced bread and a cup full of water. When I swallowed my first piece of bread, the sweetness permeated my mouth, throat, and stomach, and I knew that was my first taste of freedom. I had dreamed of living with freedom but was not physically able to taste it - American food and water. Undoubtedly, we were disheartened when the lights from the oil rig diminished into the night as we headed for our refugee camp, but we knew freedom was not too far to go, and Viet Nam was, perhaps, behind us for good.

Artist: Sudipta Steve Dasgupta

Not too long after we left the oil rig, the terrifying storm came. Initially, we moved to the lower deck for our safety with the hatch opened. The storm became explosive and violently thrashed our boat in all directions. A samurai blade of lightning severed the black boiling cloud as it struck the darkened swollen sea a few hundred yards from our boat, foreboding danger in our path. The scintillating lightning lit up the main cabin, where I could see little children were hanging on to their parents, crying, screaming, and vomiting all at once. The deafening blasts of thunder drowned out any silent prayers for mercy. The thunder tore into our fear of what could be the deadliest night in our journey, and maybe our last.

One minute the boat was tossed to the right side when it almost capsized, then it was tossed back to the left side, and then all of a sudden, it seemed as if the boat was picked up by a sea monster and slammed down into the swirling sea while a wall of water was punishing the upper deck with all its power. My head was hitting the roof of the lower deck, and my body was being jolted back and forth with each crashing wave. I saw a man on the upper deck trying to tie down the loose gear. He was almost jettisoned overboard with each jolt. After a while, the boat was trounced by an enormous amount of water, and the opening to the lower deck was nailed shut. My heart was racing with fear because one of my uncles a few years earlier perished when he couldn't escape from the lower deck. In the last few moments when our boat was being lambasted ferociously, I prayed to God for protection, and I thought this was the end for me - I crumpled into unconsciousness.

A Runaway Teenager

A bright light woke me up from what could have been the end of my life, and for a moment, I thought I was in heaven. The last thing I remembered was that our boat was about to capsize, and I was locked in the lower deck until a boy next to me nudged me to move out of the lower deck, and as I looked up, I could see a sign saying, "Welcome to Indonesia Refugee Camp" in Vietnamese. I wanted to scream out my joy and happiness, but nothing was coming out. The overwhelming pleasure paralyzed me from uttering a word out of my mouth or even moving an inch. I wasn't sure if it was real.

"We…made…it!" I stuttered to the boy who was next to me in the lower deck.

He turned and looked at me. "I know. Where have you been, you sleepyhead?" He didn't know I had passed out because of the storm.

After years of trying, multiple attempts, imprisonment, getting left behind, five nights and four days in the ocean, and the storm that took my consciousness, I was looking directly at freedom. "God has saved us," I uttered. I wish Tri could have seen it with me. He deserved this moment more than I did. I knew happiness and joy were exuding from every pore of my body, yet I couldn't put into words how I felt when I saw that sign. All of us were trying to get off the boat to celebrate. We were patting each other on the back and hugging each other.

Chapter 6

Refugee Camps

May 1980

Finally, I was free. I wasn't sure what would come next, but for now, these islands would be home for me before I could make my dream of going to America come true. Just a few days ago, I was home helping Mom with her business, praying for a moment like this, and now I was standing on the part of the road that would lead me to America. For the first time, I was alone and far from Mom and my family, but I knew God had answered my prayers. I was ready to face the challenges about to come my way.

While we were waiting to be processed, the refugees on the island gathered around us to inquire about the latest news about Viet Nam. We also discussed how they helped to land our boat at the right place. When we made it past the storm, we came upon hundreds of islands, and there was no lighthouse to help us. The captain realized that we were in the back of the islands, but he had to see the islands from the front to see the camp. He drove our boat between the two islands, even though the current was powerful, then turned the boat back to look for lights. He found the lights to the camp, but he did not know how to come in safely because of rocks and shallow water. Some boats tried to go in without help, but they crashed, and lots of people died. We made loud noises and lit up a torch to alert the people on the island, seeking their help to dock our boat. When the people on the island heard the noise from our boat, they lit up a bonfire to guide us away from the rocks. The captain followed the light from the island and landed our boat safely. I wished I had been awake to witness the dramatic docking.

Indonesia has thousands of islands. Kuku was one of the islands used to shelter refugees, starting in 1979. The remnants of the broken shelter left behind from previous refugees allowed us to piece together as many shelters as possible while waiting for our next destination. We were given food, water, and a prepaid envelope to write home. I wrote to Mom immediately to let her know that I made it. I pictured how happy Mom and my siblings would be when they saw an envelope with a stamp from Indonesia come to the door. My friends from the neighborhood would soon find out I had made it out of Viet Nam for good - no more making fun of me for trying.

My family and I didn't know what the future would be for us, but for now, at least one of us made it out. Kuku was beautiful and majestic. The cove was shaped almost like a "U," with rocks on both sides of the island. The jungle was behind us, and the ocean was just a few hundred feet from our shelters. Every evening people gathered in small groups down the beach to talk, play guitar, smoke, and watch the moon. I made my way to the beach almost every night to listen to the people reminisce about their lives and how they got out of Viet Nam. Sometimes, I sat at the beach late at night to watch out for boats like ours.

For all the time I was in Kuku, we didn't see a single boat come to the island. There wasn't much to do on the island while we were waiting for our next destination. However, one afternoon when I ventured into the woods out of curiosity, I was bitten by this giant, black, furry spider. I endured a fever and a swollen hand until it went away a few days later. Homesickness and loneliness visited me quite frequently. I was farther away from home than I had ever been. I wanted to swim back to Mom, but I knew that was not feasible. I realized that I was indeed far away from Viet Nam. It would have helped so much if Tri was there with me; at least we would have had each other. But I had to face the inevitable on my own. I cried myself to sleep a few nights.

We were fortunate enough to wave goodbye to Kuku after a brief stay, and we were moved to a more desirable island, Galang. I didn't think I could step on another boat so soon, but this boat was a thousand times bigger than our boat and was well equipped with the necessary floating devices if a rescue operation was needed. The boat was large enough to walk from the upper deck to the lower deck freely without any physical limitations. However, the memory of being on the lower deck during a dreadful storm was still lurking in my subconscious, so the upper deck was my only choice. We were fed ramen noodle soup, which was the best food I had had in a long time.

This island was made up of two parts for refugees - Galang 1 and Galang 2. Our boat ended up in Galang 1. On this island, a lengthy and detailed process began to help each refugee settle to his or her final destination or "third country."

Galang was designed to accommodate thousands of refugees. The island was distinctive from Kuku upon our arrival. A concrete pier for the boat to drop off the passengers seemed official. There were larger structures to accommodate the refugees coming from Kuku. I was surprised to see cargo trucks and small cars along the dock waiting to take us to our new home. The roads to our shelters were curvy but paved. I was happy to smell the mixture of diesel and cigarettes once again. Homes of the denizens scattered along the road, displaying how habitable the island was. However, most of the island was covered with big trees and bushes. It was a forest for me. Galang would be my home until I was able to move to my third country.

A little more than a hundred barracks were built to shelter the refugees on Galang 1. A small group of us were given barracks number 103. Inside each barracks, four even sections were made of wood and elevated to my hip level, and each barracks came with four bathrooms and an area for the kitchen. Mr. Six's group, including me, took one side of the barracks, while the other group on the boat took the other side. The boat owner's family was given the barracks next to us.

We were given one bag of food per person per week. Each bag included a can of spam or chicken, a small bag of salt, sugar, black pepper, some soy sauce, cooking oil, and approximately one pound of rice. In the beginning, for the food to last the entire week, we put our food together and ate in a big group. After a few months, we broke up into smaller groups to fend for ourselves. We often ran out of food before the week was over, so we supplemented by growing vegetables in the back of the barracks. We also received one gallon of water per day for all purposes, and we used empty oil barrels to collect rainwater for showering, cooking, drinking, and anything else that we needed.

There was electricity for the streetlights, hospital, and official buildings, but not for our barracks. It seemed as if the island was functioning as a small city. There was a Catholic Church located a short distance from my barracks. I enjoyed it whenever I went to church because an Italian priest did mass in Vietnamese. There was a Buddhist temple located on top of a hill. A little shopping center was just a few hundred feet from my barracks. Sundries were sold, and I couldn't believe that they even had *phở* - Vietnamese beef noodle soup. I visited the post office almost every day, hoping for a letter from Mom. There was a library for us to learn English and even a school for little kids.

The first few months on the island were testing - especially for me and the other unaccompanied minors. We knew, however, this was only a temporary stay. The final destination was waiting for us. During the day, there were things for us to do to keep our minds occupied, but when the night came, the music from the coffee shop talked about the boat people; it was meaningful yet sorrowful at the same time. It was hard for me not to think of home. I sat on the edge of the window, waiting for the music to come on every night. I preferred to enjoy the free music by myself due to my unprosperous status.

Mr. Six and his wife eventually moved to the school where she taught the little kids, and our group became smaller, all boys. A couple of months after we were situated on the island, we discovered a beautiful beach not too far from our barracks, but we had to cut through the jungle to get to it. Every evening after we made our dinner, we went to the beach for our daily swim. The mosquitoes were unforgiving, but we got used to them. The beach was so beautiful and inviting almost every day. The sand was as white as an unpainted canvas. The water was crystal clear and blue like the sky in the springtime. Coconut trees swung out to the edge of the water. We thought we were in a postcard. We knew the chance of us returning to this island once we settled in our third country was implausible, but in the meantime, we swam, frolicked, and played to our heart's content until it was time to come back for our daily dinner with spam awaiting us. Most of the time, we ate spam for dinner. Occasionally, we would get sardines in the can, and that was a treat. I had no complaints about the food that was given to us; at least we had food.

People who made it to Galang would wait for the immigration office to interview them for their third country. One by one,

Refugee Camps

each boat would be interviewed when their turn was up. While waiting for the interview, we were recruited to immigrate to Canada and Europe. We could leave the island within a few weeks. Some people made a dash for the opportunity to leave the island behind, eager to start a new life. Nothing could entice me away from my America.

It was easier to settle in Canada, Europe, and Australia than in the United States of America. The majority of us wanted to go to America since America was the freest country in the entire world. It took a long while before our boat was interviewed. Most people were being interviewed for their migration to the US. However, getting into the US was extremely difficult. Some people were interviewed multiple times and still weren't able to get into the US. They eventually gave up and took the offer to go to Canada or Europe.

There was talk about what to say and how to say things to earn a place in the US. Many of us learned about America from the people who made it there. My uncle, my mother's younger brother, made it to America in 1975 with his entire platoon when Sai Gon fell. He had written Mom a few letters and even sent her gifts and photos of America. We read his letters so many times that after a few months, those letters were so wrinkled that they were unreadable.

Freedom of religion is genuinely exhibited in America. My uncle wasn't being watched on Sunday when he went to church. There was no interference from the government for wearing long hair or bell-bottom pants. The money he made he could keep without worrying about it being taken away. All kinds of books, music, and literature were allowed to be enjoyed. The neighbors weren't spying on him for authorities. These fundamental freedoms were usurped from us. We found America to be the place that would and could give us these freedoms. We called America the promised land, and we would trade our lives for it.

The people on our boat were interviewed after about six months on the island. I was excited and nervous; this interview was the key for me to enter my promised land. On the day of the interview, we were gathered under a larger canopy right below the interviewer's bench, where we could look up and see both the interviewee and the interviewer together. When my name was called, I ran up the steps quickly. I was told to sit down in front of an American person and an interpreter.

"What is your name?"

"Quyen Ha, sir."

"And how old are you?"

"Fourteen, sir."

"Do you have any relatives in America?" I hesitated for a moment. I knew if I admitted that I had an uncle in America, they would try to reunite me with my uncle. With a bad history of living with relatives, I didn't want to be united with him.

"No, sir."

"Quyen, why do you want to come to America?"

I pondered for a few seconds. The question was easy, yet it was profound. Who wouldn't want to come to America? I didn't know what he was looking for, but I knew the reason for me to trade my life for America.

"Freedom," I replied, looking straight at him without blinking.

"What do you know about freedom?" he asked contemptuously. "You're only fourteen years old."

Everything came back to me in a flash. "Under the communist regime, there was no freedom. People were being watched for what they said and did. They had to ask for permission to travel from one place to another. The rich people were treated as monsters; their wealth was taken away from them in front of their eyes. Music and books from the previous regime were deemed unhealthy for the mind. Ergo, they were banned or destroyed. People couldn't wear clothes that were considered inappropriate or too Western. Hair got cut off on the street if it was too long. And if you don't believe me, you should try to living in Viet Nam as a citizen for one year."

With that, he smiled. "Raise your right hand, kid."

I rushed down to the bench where the rest of the people had been watching me from below, and they were ecstatic when

A Runaway Teenager

they saw me raise my right hand to swear in for entrance to the United States of America. But most importantly, they wanted to know what I said to be able to qualify for America. I told them to tell the truth. They cheerfully nodded their heads in agreement. Most of the people in our boat made it through the first step to migrate to America that day, and some of them even left the island before I did. I ran down the hill and went back to the barracks. All the while, I was thinking about my family. I knew Mom would be thrilled to know my first crucial step was completed.

As people slowly left the island to settle in their third country, my group faded away. I found another small group to share food with, and when that group was gone, I would look for another group to join in the barracks. There was a place for unaccompanied minors to stay, but by the time I found out about it, I was happy to stay with the people in our boat. Before Mr. Six's departure, his youngest daughter told me an interesting story about our trip. She recalled that there were multiple attempts to escape, but they couldn't go. Her dad was concerned, and he sought advice from his older daughter, who was reading tarot cards, to see why he could not escape the country successfully. The tarot cards told her that there was a kid that her father must not forget so that he could escape safely. I didn't think his youngest daughter knew that kid was me. Mr. Six and his family settled in Australia.

The quickest way for the refugees to get to America was to be sponsored by their relatives, or an unknown family in

America could sponsor them. In the '70s, '80s, and even up to the mid-'90s, many American families were willing to help bring Vietnamese refugees from the refugee camps to America. Another quick way to come to America, in my case, was to join the unaccompanied minor housing in the camp. These minors were to be fast-tracked to the third country as soon as possible. Initially, I wanted to be sponsored by an American family, so I lied about my uncle in America in my first interview. Languishing as refugees in Galang wasn't conducive for many people, but with freedom and God's help, I could survive anything that life threw at me. Not too long ago, I was being tossed in the ocean until I blacked out, and this thought comforted me.

To my surprise, the people in my boat were leaving in droves. There was more space in the barracks for me to enjoy. While I was waiting for my turn to settle in my third country, I spent a lot of time discovering the island. I was so glad to find some people from the same city in Viet Nam, and we often got together. While I was roaming the island, I met Victor, who had been on the island before I came. Victor was a few years older. We both left our family behind. Our friendship developed rapidly, perhaps because we both were alone.

I also found a job baking bread. My job started around midnight, and I baked bread until early morning. In the morning after my job, I would go to the library to learn English by listening to an English conversation between two people while looking at the written dialogue. I fell asleep every time I listened to the tape. The library had fifteen tapes, and it seemed as if people were finishing these tapes very quickly, and I was still on tape one every time one of the students asked me how far I had listened. The people in my barracks threatened me that if I didn't pass the English test, I would not be able to leave the island. I was worried about that, but there was never a test to take.

A year went by, and I got my second interview. They asked me if I had a relative in America; I said no again. I didn't know my mother had written to my uncle and asked him to bring me to the States. My third interview came a few months later, and again, they asked if I had a relative in America; I said no. This time they told me I had an uncle in America, and he had sponsored me. Mom had sent letters to my uncle and informed him of my presence in Galang. I agreed with the immigration officer about the arrangement. One and a half years after I arrived in Galang, I heard my name over the PA system announcing that I was scheduled to leave for America. All the people in the barracks were so happy to know another person was leaving for America but sad that it wasn't their turn. I knew how they felt about watching other people go. It was finally my turn to come to America.

America. The land of freedom that I had dreamed of for so long. The land so many of us had traded our lives for. And the land that I would call my country. I wondered what America would be like.

Victor took me to the port and got our picture taken by a photographer. I didn't know how he was going to pay for it. I couldn't give Victor my address in America because I didn't know it, and Victor didn't have a sponsor by the time we said goodbye. We made a pact to look for each other if we could and pray that we would find each other again. I took my last walk to the port to depart for Singapore, then to America. I waved back to Victor and the people who stood on the dock just when the boat pushed off from the pier, and tears came down my face. I felt fortunate to be the one leaving the island, yet remorseful for those who stayed. I stood on the back of the boat until Galang was just a tiny spot.

Chapter 7

Coming to America

December 1981

With a view at thirty thousand feet from the window seat, I felt as if I was so close to God that I could reach through the blue sky to touch him and thank him that I was finally free. A Boeing 747 carried a few hundred refugees, including me, from Singapore to California. It was a great comfort to know that this journey did not require a boat and water. I had had enough boats and water for a lifetime. I was elated and overwhelmed with the trip. At fifteen years old, my dream of coming to America was twenty-four hours away from becoming a reality, and this time there wouldn't be any guns or cops to stop us. Joy, happiness, and excitement were dancing in my heart. The feeling could only be felt by those who had found freedom after an incredulous journey. I closed my eyes to let the euphoria dissolve inside my body - knowing that I was free at last.

I couldn't help but ruminate about the events that brought me to the door of this airplane, and I was so grateful that God was there for me. I knew it wasn't my footprints because he was carrying me every step of the way. It wasn't too long ago that I was about to perish in the stormy sea, and now I was flying on an airplane to my third country. The pleasantry of appreciation, hope, and aspirations from my fellow travelers about America brought me back to reality. I could hear, feel, and see how grateful we were to America for giving us a chance to live in freedom. All of us were living in a dream.

We landed in Oakland, California, around midnight, and it took a long time for customs to process all of us. The cold air caressed my face gently as I stepped outside the airport to catch my bus for the refugee camp, attesting that I was no longer in Southeast Asia. I knew that was the air of freedom welcoming me to a new life in this great country. Until that moment, I had never experienced cold weather in my life. I let the cold air cuddle my face and body until it was time for me to get on that bus. We were bused to Hamilton Refugee Camp around three in the morning. Although it was early in the morning, the streets of America were more impressive than I had thought.

I was shocked to see that there were lights on the streets; they were lane reflectors. They even had lights inside the bus. Homes and buildings were lit with lots of lights. There were no cops on the streets to stop people from wearing bell-bottom pants or stop people who had long hair. There were cars on the road at that early hour, indicating that there were no curfews. And no vendors were chasing us down to sell their delectable goods. The bus ride was my first glimpse into the future in America. I was in awe with what I saw just through this bus ride. The pictures I saw of America from my uncle didn't do justice to what I saw on that bus ride. America was so beautiful. She was more glorious than what I had imagined in my dreams. If this was so magnificent, I knew the best of America was awaiting me. My heart was dancing with joy and happiness, and I thought of Tri and wished he was here to soak in what freedom was like in America.

At the refugee camp in America, we were given room and board while we were waiting for our new home. There was a donation center for us to find some clothes because it was freezing. I found a jacket to keep warm and a pair of boots that nobody wanted. Those boots were too big for my feet. They made me look like Charlie Chaplin, but I loved them. My uncle came with his friends a few nights later to meet me. When I saw him, I ran and gave him a big hug. He told me he would pick me up the next day.

We spent about two weeks in California with my uncle's friends Mr. and Mrs. Nguyen. They took me to some of the most beautiful places that I had ever seen. Up in the mountains where I saw and touched snow for the first time, the snow was soft and powdery. I frolicked in the snow for the first time in my life. My uncle and his friends joined in the fun.

Mr. and Mrs. Nguyen lived in a big Vietnamese community. There were many Vietnamese restaurants and markets. Some street names were in Vietnamese. There were banks with

A Runaway Teenager

Vietnamese owners. We even saw a movie in a Vietnamese theater. People could live here without speaking English. I was intrigued by what I saw and learned. The Golden Gate Bridge was enormous and magnificent. I had seen bridges in Viet Nam, but they couldn't compare.

My uncle took me to Chinatown in San Francisco, and I thought I was back in Viet Nam except there were no cops. I could tell people were living in freedom. Prosperity was all around the city, and the economy's engine was pumping at high speed. Buildings were as tall as the eye could see, and cars were omnipresent in the streets. The people seemed happy as they went about their lives. I was so pleased to see how people harmonized in this freedom that God had given them.

Before we left for my uncle's home in Texas, my uncle asked me if I wanted to stay in California with his friends, whom I hardly knew. I just saw my uncle, and we had had little time to visit or live together. I decided to go to Texas with my uncle. The drive from California to Texas was an introduction to the partial landscape of America that I had always wanted to experience. I stayed up as much as I could to soak in America that I had imagined. The desert was intimidating and amazing at the same time. There was no civilization for miles, and the darkness could only add to my anxiety. What was lurking behind those mountains? When we got to Texas, the highways were more populated than those of other states, and yet it was still a long way from home.

My uncle lived in Austin, deep in the heart of Texas. I wanted to share as much as I could with my uncle about Viet Nam, my trip, and my refugee camp. However, my uncle was in great distress much of the time. He had just broken up with his girlfriend. Now he had to take care of a boy whom he had never seen before. There was so much work to do for a new refugee in America, including medical checkups, school enrollment, follow-up with the local immigration office, and various items required to be done within a few months in the new country. My uncle was working full-time, and it was hard for him to take off work to take care of me. I felt terrible for my uncle because his life had changed from a single lifestyle to living like a father with a son. I wanted my uncle to be happy with me, but I felt like I was a burden. Nevertheless, my uncle did the best he could to take care of me. I was forever grateful for his rescue.

My uncle lived in a two-bedroom apartment not too far from the main street. He gave me one of the rooms. I thought that was too much for one person, especially when we used to have one room for five or six of us. My uncle's friend Henry helped to enroll me in high school the following spring. Henry was very friendly and took care of me. On one occasion, Henry bought fried chicken. I was so excited! When the food came, I had almost half a chicken to myself, and suddenly I thought about my brothers and sisters, who were still foraging for food most days. Life in America was coming to me at a fast pace, and it was tough for me to control my emotions at times.

A Runaway Teenager

It was challenging to start school with a brand new language, but I was not afraid and eager to start this journey. My uncle bought me a Vietnamese-English dictionary to assist me, and by the end of the first semester, the dictionary was unrecognizable. One of the classes was ESL - English as a Second Language - and when I got to the class, I felt comfortable right away because there were other Vietnamese students.

Cory, who was in this class, became one of my best friends. David, the teaching assistant to our ESL teacher, later became my "adopted" brother. He had a unique ability to communicate and teach the English language. All of us became friends with David. Most of the subjects required lots of English, but math was more straightforward for me to understand. The American kids were kind and accommodating whenever possible. I loved school and was ready for it every day. I wanted to learn English as fast as I could. Ms. Kim was a Vietnamese lady who helped me translate whenever the school administration needed to talk to me about the necessary paperwork. I walked to school every day because my uncle's apartment was close to the high school - one less thing for my uncle to worry about.

A few weeks in, school became a routine for me. I walked to school in the morning, and my uncle went to work. When I came home, my job was to cook the rice with the rice cooker. One time, I left the apartment to meet up with Cory, and I forgot to push the button to cook the rice and left the keys in the door when I left the apartment. My uncle was not happy about the keys being left in the door. I knew that didn't help the burden that was mounting with every mistake I made.

Whenever I was out with Cory, I asked permission from my uncle. Cory was living with his uncle when we met. He escaped out of Viet Nam with his uncle. His dad didn't come with him, and his mom died of a dog bite when he was young. We were in a similar situation. Most Fridays, when school was out, we would walk about five miles to the mall. Sometimes we played video games, but we didn't even know when the game was over. On occasions, the manager felt bad and put a few quarters in for us. We also hung out at the ice-skating rink to watch people skate. David would join us at the mall whenever he was available. For the time being, high school was fun and comforting. There were two meals a day, and the food was so good, but I could hardly enjoy it because the thought of my family being hungry was still on my mind. I found great comfort whenever I was able to talk to Cory. One Friday, when we were on our way to the mall, I wasn't feeling well about things at home with my uncle, so I wanted to know if Cory had the same problem.

"Hey, Cory. How is it living with your uncle?"

"Well, I feel uncomfortable at times. I feel as if it's not my family. He has lots of kids, and I like my cousins and all, but it's not the same."

"Have you ever thought about living with someone else?"

"Sometimes, when things don't go right, I want to leave the house and be on my own."

"What kinds of things don't go right?" I probed a little.

"I better not say anymore. Let's not talk about me. What about you with your uncle?" he asked with concern on his face. "You don't look so happy today."

"I feel as if I am a burden to my uncle. He works hard all day and has to take care of me when he gets home, and I feel he is not happy with me."

By now, my family and friends knew I was living with my uncle in America. I was communicating with my family and friends in Viet Nam by letters. I confided in them about my feelings, that I was a burden to my uncle. I also wrote to a friend from the boat who was living in California. He wrote back and asked me to move to California with him. However, my uncle found these letters, and he was unhappy about what I told my friend. I was forbidden to write to Viet Nam or my friend in California if I wanted to live with him. I apologized and promised not to write to Viet Nam anymore. I felt miserable for not writing to Mom and friends, but I respected my uncle and was so grateful for his help that I obliged.

"What did you say to your friend that made him ask you to move in with him?" my uncle asked angrily.

"I just told him that I feel as if I was bothering you, and I am not sure that you are happy with me. That was all," I cried.

"From now on, you are not allowed to write to anyone, your friends or your family in Viet Nam, if you want to live with me," he shouted, and his face was red. I could see the anger in his face, and I was scared.

"Yes, Uncle. I am very sorry for the trouble I have caused," I continued to cry.

Chapter 8

My American Family

March 1982

By the end of my first semester in school, my uncle moved us out of the two-bedroom apartment to an efficiency, not too far from the previous apartment. With the new place, Cory and I could not see each other very much, and our Friday trip to the mall had stopped. Luckily, David was able to hang out with me from time to time when he had the car.

One evening when David and I were outside the apartment, my uncle came home with his friends, and from the way they looked and sounded, I knew they were inebriated.

"Quyen, I am home," my uncle slurred. He walked into the apartment, supported by his friends. They were cursing and screaming incoherently. None of them were able to stand up straight. I flashed back to the time in Viet Nam when I witnessed some violence from drunk people. They beat up their kids, their wives, or their neighbors. I didn't want to be around my uncle when he was drunk, afraid of what he might do to me. Luckily, David was there with me, so I wasn't alone.

"David, I can't stay here. Can I spend the night at your home?" I asked.

"Of course," he replied. We rushed out of the apartment without saying anything to my uncle.

The next day David took me back home to gather my things and run away from my uncle. I was hoping my uncle would be at work, but he was at home. My uncle came out of the bathroom while I was gathering my things in the apartment.

"If you had made it home last night, I would have killed you," he said calmly.

I was shocked to hear that, but I knew it wasn't the alcohol talking. I was right for not staying the night in the apartment. One thought that was going through my mind was that if the ocean didn't kill me, I was certain I didn't want to be killed by my uncle.

"You don't have to worry about me anymore. I am leaving," I told him as I took the keys from my pocket and left them on the table.

I suspected that this day would come, but I didn't think it would arrive so soon. I ran out of the apartment quickly lest my uncle carried out his wishes. I sat quietly in David's car and couldn't believe I just ran away without knowing what would happen to me. I felt as if the runaway movie started again with me, but this

My American Family

time in a different country. David took me to his home, and I asked his mom if I could stay for a while. In the meantime, I tried to find some money to go to California to live with one of my friends from the boat.

David's mom was generous and loving. She took me in with open arms. I asked for two weeks; I got almost three years. Mama was a single parent with three kids - David, Chris, and Erin. They treated me with love and kindness. I began my life with my new family, the one I dreamt of in camp. My "adopted" brothers and sister helped me with my English and treated me like a long-lost brother. They complained about Mom's cooking at times, but I loved it. She accidentally burned some food one time, and I ate it because I liked my food a little charred. From then on, Mama would try to burn a little for me.

I did whatever chores I could to help Mama: mowing the grass, doing dishes, and occasionally cleaning out the garage. Living with Mama was very peaceful, but I still feared that my uncle would find out where I lived and hunt me down for whatever reason. Even though Mama's home was farther from the school, I still walked to and from school every day.

A few months after living with Mama, a man came to the house to ask questions about me. He talked to Mama for a long time. I tried to eavesdrop on their conversation, but I couldn't understand it. One of my concerns was if my uncle had had something to do with it. He came almost every month for a while, and he usually stayed about an hour. Mama explained to

A Runaway Teenager

me that he was from the "social service office." I didn't know how he was able to track me down, but he did. Mama did not have the proper paperwork as an "adopted" mother, so the social service office was checking on Mama monthly. Mama told me she didn't care if they came every day because she loved me and wanted to help me. The idea of people checking on me brought more fear than comfort to me. The last thing I wanted in the freest country in the world was to be tracked by the government.

Our house was in a corner lot. There were enough rooms for all of us. There was laughter in our home most of the time - except when we were misbehaving, and Mama would crack the spatula to warn us. One evening Mama went to check on me to say goodnight, but she didn't see me in bed. She went berserk and woke everyone up to look for me. They looked inside and outside the house but couldn't find me. Mom came back to my bedroom and looked again. This time, she found me sleeping on the floor. She asked why I slept on the floor. I was missing home. I thought of my family sleeping on a concrete floor; sleeping in a comfortable bed didn't feel right. Mama understood and never told me where to sleep. I slept on the floor most of the time. She told me I could share anything with her whenever I needed to. Mama did what she could to help me. She cut my hair with a bowl. I didn't think that was possible, but Mama did it. She placed a bowl on my head and cut around the edge of the bowl. My siblings laughed at Mama and me, but I was happy with it. I took any help I could. Mama's friends gave me some used clothes to wear. I was grateful for their support.

The summer when I was sixteen years old, I found a job as a janitor in my high school. I made three dollars and twenty cents an hour, the minimum wage at the time. When I got my first paycheck, I sent Mom one hundred dollars, and I was so delighted when she got the money. Some relatives in Viet Nam accused me of stealing money from my uncle in America. I didn't think they knew that I was no longer living with my uncle. The family was happy for some relief, but Mom was concerned for me. She didn't want me to jeopardize my education by working. I promised Mom when I made it to America that my number one goal was to get an education. I knew making money was important, but I didn't dare break my promise to my mother. Mom never asked me for money, and she didn't allow anyone in the family to write to me for money.

When the summer was over and school started again, I worked part-time as a dishwasher at a cafeteria at the mall. A great benefit as a dishwasher was for me to clean up the leftovers, and very often, I was able to eat the leftovers from the food bar without the manager knowing. We weren't allowed to eat the leftovers. A few months after I started working in the cafeteria, it was time for me to reapply for the government assistance that my uncle had applied for when I first came to America. The social worker asked if I wanted the assistance for fifty dollars a month, and if I took the assistance, I couldn't work. I told the social worker that I appreciated the help, but now that I could work to help myself, I would like to continue to work.

A Runaway Teenager

High school was fun and exciting for me. The teachers were kind and accommodating. When I raised my hand to answer a question, I didn't get punished or ridiculed for being wrong, which happened in Viet Nam. The teachers would stay after school to help us if we needed help with our homework. There was lunch provided for us daily. Some students complained about the food, but it was comestible for me. It wasn't long ago that I was eating spam daily for almost a year and a half. Usually, around midday, we were allowed to play sports for one hour.

When I was seventeen, I told Mama that I would like to move out of the house, and she agreed. I wanted to be independent and provide for myself, but I didn't realize how much it took to live independently. An older friend who tried to help me let me live with him for a while, and he was also a friend of my uncle. I moved in with him in the same apartment that I lived in with my uncle a few years back. The relationship didn't last long. I moved in with another friend from high school in the same apartment a few weeks later. Sharing a room with other high school students could be deleterious to my health. People were going in and out of the apartment at all hours. The older kids were drinking daily. And when drugs were offered to me for the first time, I knew it was time for me to get away from these friends. Using drugs was the one thing Mom had inculcated me not to do before I left for America. Her sage advice came to me as if she was standing next to me when those drugs passed around in the room. Those people weren't happy with me when I refused to do drugs with them. Life was more demanding on my own, but I was determined not to disappoint the people who helped me get to where I was. My uncle often told me I would never make it to the school I wanted to attend, the University of Texas at Austin. His negative words only inspired me to work harder.

After the immigration office in Austin discovered that I was no longer living with my "adopted" mother at seventeen, they arranged for me to go to court and obtain an emancipation document to live by myself without adult supervision. I could sign any paper that required my parent's signature from school. The judge advised me that this piece of document was for me to be on my own legally, but not for me to buy alcohol. I promised the judge I would live my life judiciously. This piece of paper saved me from harassment from my uncle when he found out I was living with his friend. The Austin Vietnamese community was tiny in the '80s. When word got out that I was living with my uncle's friend, he came fuming. Maybe it was an embarrassment for him that I chose to live with his friend. I was scared, but I told him I could live independently, and I showed him the emancipation document; he never bothered me again.

Cory and I ran into each other a few weeks after the party at my apartment. He had moved out of his uncle's home a couple of months earlier. He never told me why, and I never asked, although I could imagine what it was like to live with relatives. When our visit ended, I asked Cory if I could share a room with him. Cory and his brother were kind enough to let me share a

A Runaway Teenager

one-bedroom apartment about one block from my high school. I slept on the couch. Cory and his brother had the bedroom. I paid for rent and food with the money I earned. I quit my dishwasher job and found a cashier job at a gas station within walking distance from our apartment. Cory's brother had a car, so he could help us go to grocery stores and church. When Cory lost his job, I convinced Cory to work with me at the gas station.

One Christmas Eve, when Cory and I were closing up the gas station, our last customer walked up to the counter and gave us twenty dollars for Christmas. We were grateful and excited about the present. We went home, changed our clothes, and went to midnight mass with his brother. When the collection basket came to us in the middle of the mass, Cory and I looked at each other. Should we put the whole twenty in it? Or should we get change from the basket? Taking change would be a social faux pas, but twenty dollars could be Christmas dinner for three of us. While Cory and I were hanging onto the collection basket a little longer than usual, I felt as if a thousand eyes were staring at us. I looked back at Cory, and he moved his head up and down and smiled at me. I smiled back at him in agreement as I took out the twenty dollars and placed it in the basket. We went home happy and had spam for Christmas dinner. Cory and I worked at that gas station until we graduated from high school.

My high school in the '80s was ordinary, just like any other high school in Austin: guys wore polo shirts with raised collars if they could afford it, a mullet hairstyle was fashionable, and tennis shoes with double shoelaces were in style for guys and girls. Guys with team leather jackets were a magnet for cute girls. Never mind the cute girls, I just wanted the leather jacket. Acquiring the jacket was easy. I needed to join the soccer team, to which I was invited to be a team member. However, joining the team required me to spend more time after school, and I had a job after school. Food and rent were more critical, so the team jacket was not desirable after all. From time to time, I stopped by the practice and watched my friends for a few minutes before work to cheer them on or live vicariously through them. I never felt envious or jealous of my friends who had parents that were able to provide for them. I always thought I was given so much - freedom - and a small childhood desire could be relinquished for a better tomorrow.

During the summers, in addition to working at the gas station, I was fortunate enough to get a summer job at IBM through a summer job program for high school students. The people at IBM were so kind and generous to me. My boss, Mr. C, took time after work to help me with my homework from time to time, and he helped me keep my job there every summer. I can never forget what they had done for me.

Chapter 9

Dreams Coming True

August 1985

When I left Viet Nam, one of my goals was to sponsor my family to America. I knew the process would take at least ten years. One of the requirements was that I had to be a US citizen, which I could obtain after living in America for seven years. First, I had to get a green card; it was easier to get after three years of living in the US. But the sine qua non of all was that I couldn't have a record with the police. I was determined to do everything in my power to comply with the law to achieve my goals. I avoided drugs and alcohol at all times, and I chose my friends very carefully. In the meantime, I would need to do my part to graduate from high school, and if I was lucky enough, I could attend the University of Texas in Austin.

Ever since I found out that I could be a US citizen after living in America for seven years, provided I followed all the rules, I made my number one goal to obey the law. To live in America as a refugee was prodigious, but to become a citizen was an honor that I would treasure for the rest of my life.

A Runaway Teenager

In 1985, I graduated from high school, and I was fortunate enough to be accepted to the University of Texas in Austin to an engineering program. Going to college was momentous for me, considering five years earlier, I was surviving the refugee camp. I didn't know why I wanted to be an electrical engineer; perhaps it was the zeitgeist in town. People were making great money with this degree, and the job was easy to find. Although I had to borrow money to pay for my education, it was vital for my family and me. My first year in college was grueling, but I made it through. I continued to work and do whatever I could to support myself through college.

Along the way, I met some fantastic friends in college. These friends had a significant influence on me. They helped me by giving me their time and money. I was forever grateful for their help. I would never forget what they did for me. This debt I could never repay. They would all be a part of helping my family to America, eventually.

I met Teresa, my first girlfriend, my first year in college. She was loving and supportive of what I was going through with my college life. I wouldn't have made it without her help through those tough years in college. Her whole family was very kind to me and supportive of me. But my immature nature caused many problems between us, and I wish I had done better in our relationship. I prayed that those were venial sins.

Teresa introduced me to Mr. and Mrs. Howard. They were a loving couple. Mr. Howard was one of the best attorneys in

Austin, and Mrs. Howard was a chief household officer. The old adage seemed to ring true in this case - behind every great man there was a great woman. She put him through law school. At the end of every semester, they invited us to their home for dinner. They cared for us as if we were their children, which they didn't have. We enjoyed Mrs. Howard's cooking and long conversations. We listened to Simon and Garfunkel with them whenever we had a chance to visit their home.

I met John in my calculus class. He and his wife, Laura, became my lifelong friends. Laura was working as an editor for a magazine in Austin when I met her. They didn't have much for themselves, but they volunteered to help me with their time and money when I needed it the most. They were soulful people.

Pat was another dear friend who became a part of my life. I met Pat when he came to Austin for a table tennis tournament for all police departments in the country. We became friends right away. His avuncular nature made me feel protected and secure whenever I was with him. An instant bond was formed when our stories were exchanged. Pat was a sniper for the US Marine Corps who fought in the Viet Nam War. He was shot a few times and blown up a few times. The shrapnel on his body was still there to remind him of the war. I had the utmost respect and love for our armed forces. The men and women in the military were my heroes. Pat made it back to America with PTSD. The nightmare of war stayed with him for many years. Pat became a police officer for Beaumont, Texas, a few years after he made it back from Viet Nam and eventually became one of their best detectives. Pat introduced me to Susie, his wife. They were kind and gentle people who would always be there to cheer me on.

In 1988, my seventh year in America was up, and I was qualified to apply for American citizenship. The time had finally come. I was ready to complete this journey to become an American citizen. I drove to San Antonio to be tested by an INS (Immigration and Naturalization Service) agent. Throughout the process, the agent never asked if I wanted to be an Asian-American, Chinese-American, African-American, or Italian-American; his only offer was American citizenship. I accepted his offer and was glad not to be hyphenated. I knew I might not look the part or talk the part, but I knew I wanted to be one hundred percent American. I wanted to assimilate into the American way of life. I wanted to eat hamburgers, hot dogs, and apple pies. I was proud and honored when I finally raised my right hand to swear to be an American citizen a few months after passing my test. There were people from all over the world in the auditorium. When the ceremony was over, some were crying, some were laughing, and some were hugging each other, but all were proud to be called American. We all came to America for an ultimate goal - to pursue life, liberty, and happiness.

The longer I lived and learned about America, the more I learned to love her. America was an exceptional country. Its foundation of freedom allowed its people to be free to achieve the ultimate American dream. This freedom was so essential for our existence that our founding fathers were willing to sacrifice their lives, honor, and fortunes for it. The key to American exceptionalism was because of this principle - freedom. Our founding fathers understood this principle, and they feared that without it, there would not be an America. On this principle alone, our founding fathers had created an exceptional country. I wasn't sure if they knew what they did for the rest of us or the rest of the world. Two hundred plus years later, millions around the world would attempt to come to America for that very principle - freedom - just as our founding fathers had hundreds of years ago. And two hundred plus years later, we are the country that the world looks up to for justice and freedom.

Chapter 10

Champ

May 1987

One Friday night, I played at the table tennis club when a young man rolled into the club in a wheelchair with his wife. I was intrigued; I had not seen a person in a wheelchair play table tennis ever in my life. Maybe it was chemistry or table tennis, but after a brief visit, we became friends immediately. Champ was looking for a place to train for his national championship games, and he found our club. I was inspired and appreciative when I learned about Champ's story. Champ was involved in a motor vehicle accident when he was eighteen years old. A drunk driver ran him over. Nothing happened to the driver, but Champ ended up in a wheelchair. Life gave Champ a lemon, and he made lemonade.

Champ didn't let his disability stop him from living a full life. Champ lived his life as an average person would and didn't ask for any sympathy. He worked as an instrument repairman for an aviation company for over twenty years. In his free time, he played discus, basketball, shot put, and any sports that he could get his hands on. He also flew single-engine airplanes until he

A Runaway Teenager

developed diabetes. When his flying days were done, he built himself a motorcycle. It seemed as though nothing could stop him from achieving his goals. I greatly admired Champ for his positive attitude and determination to live his life fully, even though part of his life was taken from him. He was confined to a wheelchair, but that didn't stop him from being the best he could be.

When I met Champ, he competed for a spot on the Paralympics team for table tennis in Seoul. I volunteered to help Champ get that spot. Because we just had a few months to prepare for the national championship games in New York, we thought it was best for me to live with Champ to train him. Teaching a person in a wheelchair is entirely different from teaching a standing person. I had to be able to see what Champ saw from his angle. It was a cumbersome task initially, but Champ was very helpful - he taught me how to teach him. Every day after work, we shut the garage door and turned off the fan so no wind could interfere with the ball. The heat was scorching in that garage, but we didn't give up or complain because we had a goal to achieve.

Every other day after practice, rain or shine, we ran. Champ pushed with his arms for six miles, and I was right next to him. One time a bad storm came while in the middle of our run. We kept on running and almost ran into an electrical wire that was knocked down from the storm. Champ was a great student. He was able to adjust what I recommended and improved quickly.

After a year of training, Champ won first place in the United States that qualified him for Seoul, and I continued to coach him. We went to Seoul for two weeks, but Champ didn't win a medal. The competition for the Paralympic athletes was fierce. I was hoping Champ could win a medal, but he was eliminated in the first round. We enjoyed being in Seoul and were grateful for the opportunity to be part of the Paralympics. I moved out of his home a few months after returning from Seoul because I wanted to be closer to the UT campus.

In the fall of 1989, I received a letter from Mom informing me that my brother Tri was diagnosed with bladder cancer, which he contracted during his imprisonment. Mom didn't want to elaborate on Tri's condition, but she asked for some medication for his cancer, and I was able to find the medicine to help Tri. I prayed to God to give Tri some time so that he could come to America for treatment. I knew Tri and my family would love America as much as I did. I didn't know anything about bladder cancer, but I suspected it was a death sentence for anyone in Viet Nam.

Even though I was working part-time to support myself, I borrowed money from friends from time to time. Some friends just gave me the money. Cory knew I was in trouble, and he gave me some money to send home whenever we hooked up. I borrowed money from Teresa until she ran out of money. I maxed out all my credit cards, and I was always behind in my payments. Financially, I was in lots of trouble, but I promised myself to pay back the money I owed all my friends one day. It would be impossible for me to bring my family to America in the current financial situation, but I wasn't smart enough to know what impossibilities were. If there was a way for me to help my family, God would help me find it.

One afternoon in November, I needed to do my laundry, so I drove from south Austin to a laundromat near Champ's home in north Austin. While waiting for my clothes to dry, I stepped outside to smoke a cigarette, and Champ just happened to drive by the place when he saw me. We were more than excited to see each other. After we came back from Seoul, Champ and I lost touch. We didn't talk to each other for a long while. I was saddened when Champ lamented that his wife had left him a few months earlier and was heartbroken. I asked Champ if I were to move back in with him, would that help heal his broken heart?

And just like that, Champ and I were back together like peas and carrots. Champ taught me how to lift weights. We ran in cold weather, in the rain, and the heat. We ran all over north Austin, even on a highway one hot afternoon - Lieutenant Dan and Forrest Gump, so we thought. People often gave us a thumbs up when they drove by us. Some even stopped and told us that we inspired them because they saw us in the neighborhood all the time. On the weekends, we stayed up late, drank cheap wine, and played our silly tunes on the piano and guitar until the wee hours of the morning.

Chapter 11

Family Coming

September 1991

I knew my family was getting closer to coming to America when I received a request from the INS to provide them with financial proof - a bank statement. Obviously, I would need money to help my family when they arrived in America. That was the last piece of paper that needed to be completed for me to see my family. I was happy but cautious. There was one problem - I didn't have any money in the bank. I needed to find someone willing to lend me ten thousand dollars for two days so I could deposit the money in the bank to obtain the letter, then take the money out to pay it back to the lender. Ten thousand dollars was a lot of money to lend to someone, even for two days.

I asked friends and anybody that I could think of to help me, but it was onerous for anybody to help with that amount of money. I knew I put some of my friends in a thorny situation by asking them for the money, but I was desperate. I maxed out all my credit cards, so there was no money to borrow, and the bank needed some collateral, which I didn't have, for a personal loan.

A Runaway Teenager

However, one last person could help: my old boss from IBM - Mr. C. Two years earlier, when I bought my first car, Mr. C co-signed for the loan. He and his ex-wife were having problems because he co-signed the loan for me. I felt so bad when I found out about their quarrel. Nevertheless, I paid off my car, and Mr. C never had to worry about me keeping my word. Fortunately, I was still working at IBM, and his office was close to mine. When Mr. C saw me in his office, he knew right away I needed something from him. I told him my situation and the plan to get the letter for the INS. He gave me a cashier's check for ten thousand dollars the next day. After I deposited the money, I asked the bank for the letter stating that I had ten thousand dollars in the bank. The following day I got the money out and gave it back to Mr. C.

A few months later, another notice from the INS informed me I needed to give them seven thousand dollars for the airplane tickets for my family to come to America as soon as possible. The wait to see my family was finally here. I couldn't believe it. I had waited eleven years to be able to see my family again. Champ and I were ecstatic with this news. But first, where could I find seven thousand dollars? This time the INS wanted cash, not a letter. I couldn't ask anybody to borrow that much money, and I didn't want to put my friends in a quagmire that could break up our friendship. Besides that, I didn't know any friends that had seven thousand dollars in the bank at any given time. I continued to pray and was optimistic that God would find a way.

One Saturday evening, Teresa and I were invited to Mr. and Mrs. Howard's home for our usual end-of-semester dinner. I told Teresa I didn't feel like going because there was so much on my mind about the INS. Around ten o'clock that evening, Teresa called and said to me that Mr. and Mrs. Howard wanted to see me the next day. She couldn't tell me what it was, and I was concerned. I thought they were unhappy because I didn't show up for dinner. I went to Mr. and Mrs. Howard's home the very next day. When I came into their home, they hugged me and asked me if I was doing all right. They said that Teresa told them I couldn't attend the dinner the night before because I was stressed about the money for my family to come to America.

I explained what the INS needed from me for my family to come to America. They wrote out a check for seven thousand dollars.

"We want to help you and your family. The money is not a loan; it's a gift," they said enthusiastically. I was flabbergasted. Not knowing what to say, I cried out loud and hugged them both. I knew it was a gift, but I made a promise to myself that I would work my hardest to pay them back as soon as I could. God had answered my prayers again.

When the INS informed me that my family would be on their way to America by the end of September, Champ and I broke down and cried joyously. I got down on my knees and thanked God for this miracle. I thought of all the people who had helped me throughout this process. I knew that without the help of my uncle, my adopted family, Teresa, the people at IBM, Mr. C,

A Runaway Teenager

Mr. and Mrs. Howard, Cory, John, Laura, and all my friends who had helped me one way or another, my family couldn't be in America. After celebrating such excellent news, Champ and I realized that we had about four weeks to get things ready for my family. My first task was to find a home big enough to shelter my mother, me, and my six siblings. Our home needed to be affordable and near a bus station so they could get around town. The other task was to buy things for the home. We bought everything for the home at a garage sale. When all my friends heard my family was coming, they all came together to help me. Some friends bought us a washer and dryer, while others were able to help with bedding or sundry items for the home, and others gave us money and time. I felt so blessed to have such beautiful friends. I would have been lost without them. A couple of weeks before my family's arrival, I was lucky enough to rent a home in central Austin with a bus stop just a few hundred feet from the front door.

A week prior to my family's arrival, my friend Pat drove to Austin with a truck full of assorted items for the kitchen. He wanted to be there to welcome my family to America. We unpacked all the things Pat had brought for the home and waited to pick up my family. The very next day, I was informed that there was a delay. I was disappointed and more concerned that the delay would be a long wait. Because we didn't know how long the delay was going to be, Pat went home. It was a disappointment for Pat. A week later, I had a final notice that my family was coming.

Family Coming

All my friends and my adopted brother David went to the airport to pick up the family. Everyone was helping to prepare for the welcoming party. Teresa prepared exceptional Vietnamese food for the party, other friends were decorating the home, and all I could do was watch with amazement. My friends didn't even know my family but were treating the event as if it were theirs. They came to witness a magical moment - a family reunited in this beautiful country. This family was not just going to embrace each other but also embrace the freedom they had dreamed of for so long.

This time my brother Tri would come to America on an airplane and not the boat, with the fear of imprisonment only a memory. Freedom had brought my friends success and happiness, and now it was time to watch another family enjoy the same prosperity. Some Vietnamese friends who were there to see my family still had families in Viet Nam. Cory's father, sisters, and stepbrothers were still in Viet Nam. I felt fortunate that my family was finally here, yet guilty because my friends couldn't experience this fortuitous event with their own families. I loved and cherished their friendship with all my heart.

We all made it to the airport half an hour early. All we could do was stand around, looking out the glass windows and chatting in happiness. All I did was think about what my mother and siblings would look like now, eleven years later. How would they react when they see me, and how would I react when I see them? Maybe Mom would knock me on the head and ask, "What took

A Runaway Teenager

you so long to bring me to America?" I laughed at the thought. I missed being able to call her "Má" - for mother.

As the airplane approached the Jetway to unload its passengers, I felt my heart pounding through my chest as if it could jump out and hug my family for me. I moved right to the door through the Jetway to look for my family when I saw the passengers. All my friends stepped aside and watched me intensely. When the passengers thinned out, I knew my family wouldn't be too far away. And then there she was. I saw a glimpse of my mother and my brothers and sisters behind the last few passengers. I took off like Seabiscuit coming out of the gate at the Kentucky Derby.

Artist: Sudipta Steve Dasgupta

A Runaway Teenager

"Má," I yelled out, then all our lives came back to me instantly as if I never left her. All the emotions I had held inside for ten years came out in one single word. My mother was born in Hue, a city located in central Viet Nam. One of the unique things about this region was its vernacular. It was beautiful and inscrutable at the same time. My grandmother was so hard to understand that every time she spoke to me, I ran to Mom for help. Mom and her parents moved to Sai Gon - a city in South Viet Nam - when she was very young. For many girls growing up in the '30s in Viet Nam, education was not desirable from their parents' point of view, though it was acceptable in society, and marriage at an early age was preferable. Mom did just that - didn't attend school and married Dad when she was very young. They moved to My Tho - a city south of Sai Gon - where Dad was stationed during his military career until the war was over.

At forty-five years old, Mom became single with many kids and not much money to her name; Mom rolled up her sleeves and went to work. She did everything that she could to make money in order to care for her kids, including being a rice dealer. She would buy rice from one dealer and turn around to sell to another dealer. Mom was a flipper even before I knew what it was. One night, there were so many customers coming to our home to buy rice from Mom that she sold all her rice in a single night. It turned out these people knew about the money exchange program from the government that would happen the next day. To spread the wealth or reduce the wealth from the people, the government would introduce a money exchange program whenever they felt the need to do it. The government would take your current cash and give you new money but at a lesser value. The old cash instantly became obsolete and unusable. The problem was the rich people and the people with connections would always know when the exchange was coming. Mom lost most of her money in one night. Some of the people who bought the rice that night were her friends. She cried a little and understood it was a legitimate transaction.

When that business failed, Mom started another business selling herbal plants to the government to make medicine. I remembered helping Mom load and unload lots of bags of dry herbal plants. When the business was doing well, Mom kept the cash she earned at home, like most people back then. One night while we were sleeping, some thieves came in and took all our cash and stole our bicycle - the only mode of transportation for our whole family. We were devastated, and it was a sad day for us. Mom walked all over town and to the black markets hoping to discover some of our stolen items. She walked around the town like a zombie in a twilight zone. Throughout the whole ordeal, I didn't see a single tear from Mom. Perhaps she was stoic for all of us. Mom didn't come home until late that evening. While Mom was out to look for our stolen items and wandering aimlessly, she passed by a church; she went in and asked God to help her to take care of her family. That was the first time Mom went to a church since she married Dad. Dad wasn't a Christian, so mom stopped going to church altogether. Mom hadn't missed a mass since that fateful day.

A Runaway Teenager

When the herbal business ended, Mom quickly found another business to start in order to take care of her family - selling baby clothes and pillowcases. Mom would carry two bags of her merchandise on a bus to a contiguous city and then walk for miles in the countryside to sell her goods. Sometimes, Mom was gone for a couple of weeks before she returned home to pick up new merchandise to sell again. All of us helped Mom by making pillowcases as much as we could. My older siblings seemed to contribute the most to help out the family.

Looking back, I wished I had been a better son, helping Mom with more chores and being more obedient instead of hanging out with friends and picking up bad habits. I didn't know how Mom was able to keep us alive through all those tough years all by herself. Day by day, Mom fought for us with all her might. When there was food, we ate, and when there was extra food, Mom would help the less fortunate in our neighborhood, and when food was scarce, we would skip a meal or two. All of us children - younger or older - knew we didn't have enough compared to other kids in the neighborhood, but we would never complain or ask Mom for things. But one thing we were always sure to ask for was freedom. We all loved and admired Mom with all our hearts, and we couldn't ever repay what she sacrificed for us. How could someone be given so little but be able to accomplish so much for her children? I promised myself that Mom would never work again when she made it to America.

I pushed many people aside when I took off and ran to Mom when I saw her first appear in the Jetway. I was sure Mom had longed to hear that very word from her son just as long, and when she heard that, she knew it was me. Mom and the rest of the family looked in my direction when they heard my voice. By the time Mom could utter a single word, my arms were around her body, and my lips were on her cheek. If a dried-up river needed to replete its water, our tears would have done the job that day. My siblings Mark, Nick, Stanley, and Lindsay were all over me. I couldn't hear anything except the sobbing of happiness.

Tri was in a wheelchair, and he was holding his Foley catheter. I cried even more when I saw him because I didn't realize Tri was quite ill for the trip. Tri was so sick that the doctor couldn't release him for the flight to America, causing the delay. Tri later told me that seven days later, when the doctor examined Tri the second time, Tri pretended that he could walk so the doctor would allow him to travel. Even though his Foley bag - a catheter that went in the bladder to drain the urine - was full of blood, he was ready to risk it all. If he had to die on the way to America, he would be glad he had tried one more time for his freedom. During the drive to our home, I couldn't speak much Vietnamese with Mom. An English word accompanied every word of Vietnamese, but somehow we were able to understand each other.

A Runaway Teenager

The party at home was joyous for all of us. We could hardly eat anything, and my family was happy to meet all my friends.

"Mom, how is Dad?" I asked at one point during the party.

"Your Dad passed away. I didn't want you to know because I wanted you to focus on your studies," Mom said calmly.

"Oh, Mom." I let out a cry that interrupted the party briefly. I felt as if I were stabbed by a knife right through my heart.

All my friends rushed to me and wanted to know what happened, and all I could say was my dad had died. Mom didn't want me to be distracted from my studies, so she didn't allow anyone in the family to let me know. I was happy to be with the family but devastated about Dad. We gathered in Tri's bedroom to eat with him when all our friends went home. We stayed up all night, celebrating our first night together. When they all went to sleep, I stepped outside, took a long drag from my cigarette, and an uneasy feeling came over me. I wondered, with a sick brother, six siblings to care for, and little money in my pocket, how would I be able to care for them? But deep down inside, I knew God would help me find a way to care for my family.

Chapter 12

Tri's Battle

October 1992

The most important thing was to take care of Tri first. Not knowing what to do with Tri, I took him to the emergency room to see if they could help us. The emergency room doctor advised us to follow up with Dr. H, a urologist. Dr. H was a kind and generous physician. Tri didn't have much money except help from the city, but he still treated Tri with compassion and kindness. Dr. H recommended a few rounds of chemotherapy. We knew this journey would be a long one, but we both were ready for it. I felt some sense of relief when I knew where to start with Tri. In the meantime, my other siblings began their journey in America. They began to learn English. A couple of months later, my younger brother and sister started working at a restaurant within walking distance from our home. My two older brothers began to work at other restaurants as well. My youngest sister had motion sickness every time she rode the bus, but she didn't give up.

The first month was grueling for me. I was struggling to take care of the family and working full-time. There were so many appointments to shuttle my siblings from one office to the next. Fortunately, some friends stepped in to help whenever they could. John and Laura would take turns bringing Tri for follow-ups with Dr. H. Cory even took my little brother to the dentist and paid for it. Champ was always helping us fix up the house. My boss at IBM was kind enough to let me take time off whenever I needed to care for my brother and gave me some money to help with the family. Life was changing rapidly. I was adjusting to living with my family, and they were learning to adjust to me, especially Mom. Mom was still treating me as her little boy. She didn't want me to date Teresa. In Viet Nam, she was able to tell me what to do, but I was Americanized and no longer in Viet Nam.

Teresa profoundly understood our situation. She often comforted me and helped me recognize that Mom was worried about losing her son. She also believed that Mom would eventually come around. I was devastated emotionally, but I made a promise to take care of Mom and the family. I also promised my siblings that I would help them through college if they chose to do so, but in either case, they must become productive citizens.

After the chemotherapy, Tri was stable enough to enjoy his life in America. I went back to UT to finish up my MIS (management information systems) degree, which I hardly used at IBM. I graduated the following year, and my boss Mr. Thomas offered me the same job with a little more money. Mr. Thomas was understanding and supportive. With the official job offer, I was able to apply for a mortgage to buy a home for my family. While we were living in the rental home, the home next door was available for purchase. The location was very conducive for all of us, so we bought the home. Even though my brothers and sister were helping me take care of the bills, I was still having financial problems from time to time. Owning the home would take more than just a mortgage, which I learned quickly after moving in.

Sometimes Mom would call me at work and ask me about not having electricity to cook. I suspected the problem, but I didn't want Mom to worry. I called the city, and they informed me that my check did not go through. For them to turn on the electricity, I had to go to the office to pay the bill. In addition to the bill, I also had to pay the penalty for writing a hot check. The bank also penalized me for insufficient funds for that check. The gas, the electricity, and the telephone were often turned off when my checks didn't go through. Eventually, Mom learned what happened when she didn't have gas, electricity, or a phone. She was wise and supportive because she knew I tried my best to care for everyone. I wanted the onus to be on me so my brothers and sister could focus on school. The financial burden was easy for me to bear, but the emotional burden was always an enemy depleting for me to defeat.

Although my mom and six of my siblings had made it to America, two of my sisters - Heather and Mary - were still living in Viet Nam. My oldest sister's husband had fought in the Viet Nam War. He and his family were eligible to come to America if he had a sponsor, so I sponsored them. A few months after my family arrived in Austin, the INS notified me of my sister's family's arrival. We were all excited and ready for their family - my sister, her husband, and their daughter. That meant I had nine people in the home to help.

The thought of caring for that many people was apprehensive, but I was ready to welcome my sister and her family to this amazing country. The same people who came to pick up my family came to see my sister's family. We had a great party. They were ready to enjoy their freedom in America. We knew it would be discommodious for all of us to live together, but we came together to make it work for everyone. Mom now only had to worry about one more daughter left in Viet Nam, who couldn't leave because she was married. My sister and her husband were diligent and ready to build their family in this great country. They began learning English. As soon as a job was available for them, they started to work. My oldest sister was having motion sickness when she took the bus, but she overcame it sooner than my little sister.

Moving right next door to my rental home was serendipitous for my cousin, the son of my uncle who brought me to Austin. One night when I came home from running an errand, I found my cousin Harold was there. Harold was sponsored to America by my uncle, but within a few months, Harold wanted to move back to Viet Nam. Initially, his dad tried to send him back with a one-way ticket, but after some convincing from the travel agent, he bought Harold a return ticket just in case Harold changed his mind.

When Harold made it back to Viet Nam, my aunts and uncles were understandably upset with his capricious decision. Why would he squander an invaluable opportunity to have a wonderful life in America? Chastened, he decided to return, but before he left, my aunts and uncles told him to look for my mother and gave him my address. When the taxi brought Harold to our old address, he was surprised that we had moved. But we only moved next door. My older brother just happened to be in the front yard when the taxi arrived. Harold came into our home and told my mother what had happened to him. Mom told him to wait for me to come home and talked to me about living with us.

After an extended visit, I told Harold he could stay with me, and I would help him as if he were my brother. I wanted to help Harold because I wanted to requite for what my uncle did for me. We often wondered what would have happened to Harold if we had moved far away from our rental home. By the time Harold moved in with us, I had eleven people in my fifteen hundred square foot home. With that many people in such a small home, the stress was unbearable when problems, issues, and quarrels arose.

A Runaway Teenager

Despite the challenges, they were nothing compared to what my mother had to deal with in Viet Nam. Tri's cancer was depleting the family's piggy bank around the time that Dad passed away. And she had a whole family to feed. Every story of how Mom had to care for the family made the problems I faced nugatory. Whatever the challenges I had to face, at least I was facing them in America. The more I learned about Mom from my siblings, the more she became my heroine. Nevertheless, I could find some comfort knowing that God wouldn't give me something I couldn't handle.

A year after Tri's chemotherapy, his cancer came back. This time he had to have his bladder removed. The news disheartened Tri, yet he determined to battle against the deadliest enemy of humankind. But he had a better chance in America than in Viet Nam. When Tri was in Viet Nam, many patients contracted similar cancer. These patients had their bladder removed and had to wear a urostomy bag. Most of these patients died of infection because of poor quality of care. A surgeon in Viet Nam recommended that Tri have his bladder removed, but the night before his surgery, Tri jumped out the hospital window and came home. It was a courageous move and a correct one. If Tri hadn't done that, I wasn't sure if he would be here in America. Dr. H advised us that he would remove the bladder and rebuild a different bladder with Tri's intestine. This way, he didn't have to wear a urostomy bag. The only thing was that Tri couldn't have kids again. Tri understood the dilemma, but he found great comfort in knowing that he already had one child. This surgery was the only way to save his life. Harold and I were with Tri through all his hospital visits. Tri's surgery went well. He came home a week later.

My oldest sister was able to find an apartment in the housing project a year after her family came to America. She later told me that living in the housing project was not safe. Drugs were rampant in her project. People were being arrested almost every weekend. And her kids were afraid to play on the swing outside her apartment. Nevertheless, the housing project was a stepping-stone for her to achieve her American dreams. She and her husband labored night and day so they could provide a better life for her children. They raised their children to the best of their ability and instilled in them the American way of life. I prayed that her children would one day see what their parents had to go through to give them this beautiful life in America. My sister and her husband saved enough money to buy a beautiful home for their family a few years later. We were so proud of her and her husband.

A few months after Tri's surgery, Mom called me to come home because there was an ambulance at our home. I couldn't understand what she was saying over the phone. My cousin Harold was in excruciating pain because his scrotum was swollen and very large, and that was the reason for the ambulance. In the ER, Harold was found to have a hernia - his intestine was falling into his scrotum. Immediately, he was required to have surgery. I stayed in the hospital with him the whole night. By now, I was so used to sleeping in the hospital recliners because of Tri's multiple hospital stays. Being sick in America, he appreciated what Tri had to go through, and I was there to help him. Harold and I became closer each day he lived with us. From the weekly trip to the grocery store to helping us fix up the house, Harold was always there to help us. We loved and cared for him, just like our own brothers. He eventually found a job and became a productive citizen in the community.

My siblings continued to better their lives in this beautiful country. Those who were able to attend school did so, and those who wanted to work had jobs. Tri even had a job making sandwiches. What little money he made, he sent it all to his wife and kid in Viet Nam. Tri even had a driver's license. Tri loved America with all his heart. He loved football, basketball, tennis, and whatever sports were on TV. But what Tri loved the most was being in the church. As soon as his health allowed, Tri joined the Vietnamese Catholic Church and played the organ for the choir. He didn't miss a single Sunday.

Tri's challenge wasn't over. Two years later, he told me his urine was bloody again. We went back to follow up with Dr. H, who recommended observing Tri's symptoms for now and to follow up with him once a month. In the subsequent visits, Dr. H apprised us that cancer had come back. The news was detrimental to our family, but Tri and I were determined to fight this battle to the end.

Not long after Tri's chemotherapy started, I was laid off from my job at IBM. It was terrible timing, but I was grateful for the years they gave me at IBM and the people I met. It was dispiriting to be fired from a job. I had been let go from IBM multiple times, but this time I knew I wasn't going to be hired back. I found great comfort in knowing God would be there for me. He took care of me in the stormy sea, and this would be nothing for God. A few weeks later, I was hired by an accounting firm with a slight raise.

With chemotherapy, there were side effects and complications that required multiple hospital visits. Tri and I were in and out of the hospital frequently. Tri lost his hair due to chemotherapy, so I shaved my hair off to let Tri know that we were in this fight together. Tri was stable for a few months after chemotherapy. One night Tri came to me and asked me why he was coughing all the time. Dr. H did a chest X-ray, and he told me that a lesion in his right lung was potentially cancerous. Additional tests needed to be done to confirm.

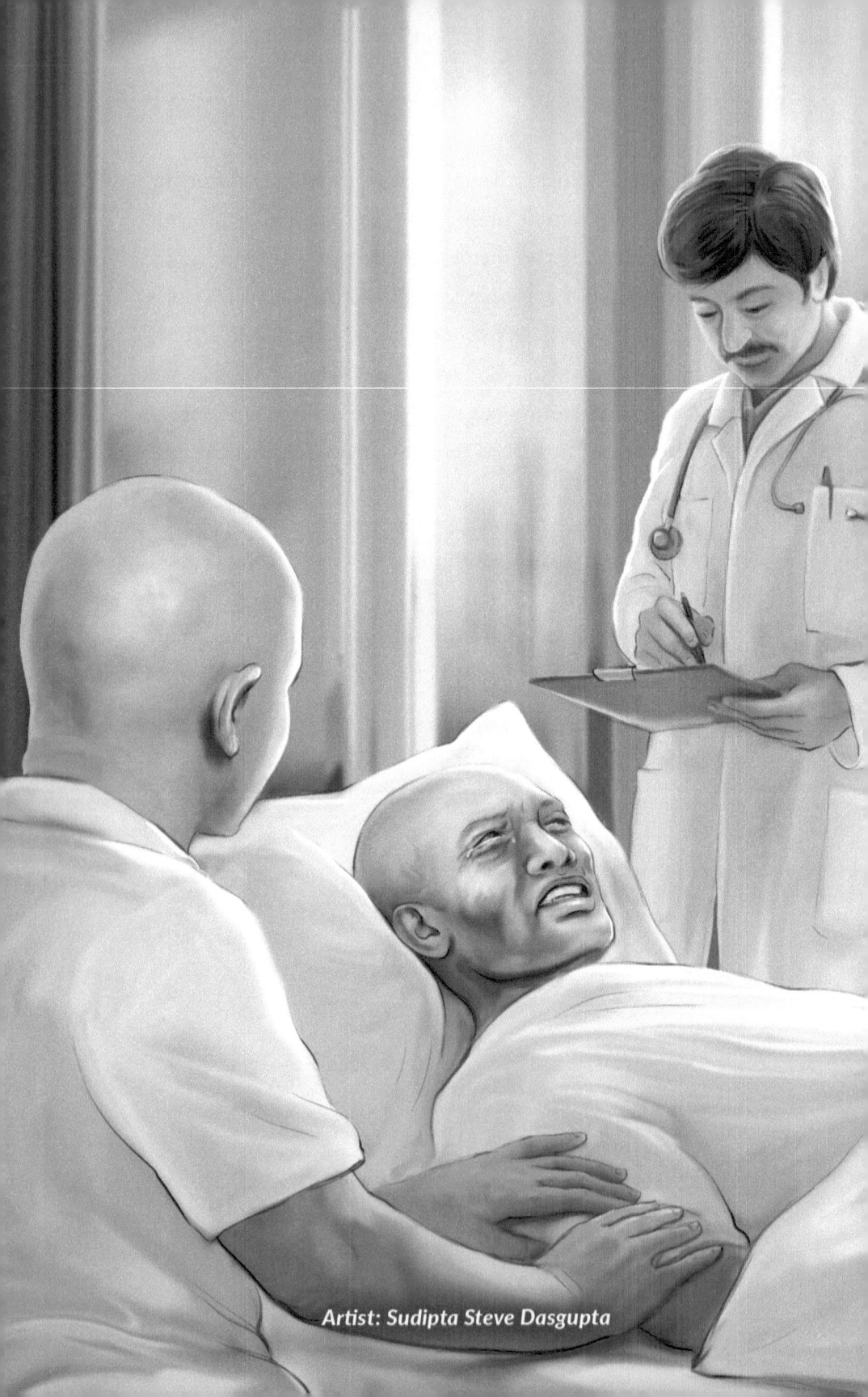
Artist: Sudipta Steve Dasgupta

Cancer in his lungs was confirmed, and Tri needed surgery. We once again went back to the hospital. Cancer had caused Tri to lose weight precipitously, so it was laborious for the nurse to find his veins. Tri's tolerance for pain was at its nadir, and with each needle stick, Tri would cry. When Tri cried, I held his hand, and I cried a thousand times. It was the first time in my life that I had to see a loved one in physical pain. With each surgery, there were complications, and with complications, the hospital stays were lengthy. Because of the language barrier, Tri was nervous being in the hospital by himself. I visited Tri every day as soon as I left work, and I stayed until he fell asleep before I went home. We would talk and play chess whenever Tri was alert. I took all my vacation days, sick days, and then nonpaid days to care for my brother. Tri was grateful for my help and said he wasn't sure if anyone in the family was capable of sacrificing emotionally, financially, or physically to do what I did for the family. I was forever grateful for his kind words, but I felt that God had chosen me for this daunting task.

About three months after Tri's lung surgery, he asked me why his left arm didn't work. I knew something was wrong. We went back to see Dr. H, and we were told cancer had made it to Tri's brain. We were referred to an oncologist, and Tri resumed chemotherapy. This time the chemotherapy took a toll on his body. Tri wasn't able to keep his food down, and he was feeling weaker every day. When the chemotherapy was done, the oncologist told us that Tri had six months to live, then walked out of the room. He didn't even allow us a few minutes to ask questions or to express our appreciation.

A Runaway Teenager

I knew my brother was sick, and deep down, I wasn't sure if he could last that long with the chemotherapy. Whether his prognosis was right or wrong at that time, we didn't know, but the way he delivered the bad news was less than compassionate. Although Tri didn't speak English, he felt the pain as much as I did when he saw the doctor's attitude. I acknowledged that he was an expert in his field, but I could have delivered the news a hundred times better than he did, and I wasn't a trained physician. I made up my mind that if I were to become a physician, I would never treat my patients that way.

We walked out of the hospital with heavy hearts. I didn't tell Tri precisely what the doctor said. Tri felt dejected. He thought the doctor wasn't kind because he didn't have money. I reassured Tri that wasn't the case. On the drive home, I struggled to find a way to tell Tri what the doctor said. How could I tell my brother he had six months to live? How could I tell anyone that they had six months to live? The news would break Tri's heart. He knew he was sick, but he was hoping for a little more time to see his wife and kid again. At the red light, before we turned into our home, I told Tri between now and the next six months, he should live as if he were going to die. He knew right away what I meant. Although Tri didn't have money, hospice took Tri in with great care. We were so blessed.

Hospice Austin was so kind and generous to Tri. For the first few weeks in hospice, Tri was able to tolerate his pain and nausea. However, Tri began to deteriorate physically, and he was required to have more vital medication to help him with his symptoms. Hospice gave us a hospital bed; we set it in our tiny little living room because that was the only place it could fit. We took turns medicating him and sleeping next to his bed to watch over him. Harold was a great help. He was always next to Tri, caring for him with all his heart. Sometimes Harold and I couldn't sleep because Tri was waking up every hour, seeing things that weren't in the room. Visual hallucinations often frightened Tri. We did our best to alleviate his fears. Some people from church came to visit Tri from time to time, but Tri was sedated by his medication most of the time.

My heart shattered as I watched my brother die a little each day. His eye sockets were forming deep cradles. His cheekbones were so prominent as if no skin or fat could be seen. And I could count every single rib on his body. I only saw this type of body in movies about concentration camps; such a body was agonizing to see on a loved one.

On the morning of January 22, 1996, I was still up from taking care of Tri all night. I looked at Tri and saw that he was breathing. I lay down next to his bed for a short nap. A few minutes later, my sister woke me up to let me know that Tri was no longer breathing. I sprung from my lying position and looked at Tri. Tri was not breathing. I thought maybe Tri just wanted me to rest before he went because I wanted to be there when he took his last breath. He was still thinking of me before he went to heaven - I thought.

A Runaway Teenager

We all came to Tri's bedside to say goodbyes. People from the church came to pray for him. It was crushing to know where to start after a person died. I didn't realize there were so many things to do for a funeral. When the funeral director came to pick up Tri, there were so many crows in the tree in front of our home, which I had never seen previously. The sky was cloudy and ominous. When Tri was still able to talk, he said he wanted to be cremated so Mom could take his body back to Viet Nam, so he could be in the old church where he used to play the organ. I didn't know how much it would cost for a funeral, but whatever Tri wanted, I would borrow money to do it for him. I had maxed out all my credit cards again by the time Tri went to be with God. We had a service for Tri in the Vietnamese church. When the service was over and the funeral home took Tri away, I ran after the hearses, wanting to tell them not to take my brother away and let me see him one last time. The hearse sped away, and I felt a pain in my heart that only a brother could feel.

A few days after the service, the choir gave me over three thousand dollars that they collected to help with the funeral, which was almost exactly how much I owed the funeral home. I honestly didn't know how I was going to pay for the funeral otherwise. I was forever grateful for their help and promised myself to pay back the choir and the church for what they did for Tri and my family. God was there for me, as always.

The accounting firm let me go after my brother died. I was surprised that it didn't happen sooner. No business could survive when the employee was taking time off all the time. I felt as if I were taking advantage of the company. My boss wanted to help me find another job in Dallas, but I told him how much I appreciated the company for allowing me to be on the payroll that long. After losing my brother, losing my job wasn't stressful for me. Losing someone I loved was more crushing than anything I had to lose. Losing Tri was wounding for all of us, especially Mom. She thought her kids would bury her, not the other way around. I couldn't imagine how tragic it was for Mom to lose her son. I knew how painful it was to lose a brother. Regular life routine was in abeyance for a while, but after that temporary suspension, moving on with our lives was a challenge. I still had a family needing my help. I was lucky that IBM called me back shortly after my brother went to heaven with a proposal to double my previous salary. God was there for me, as always.

Chapter 13

Back to School

August 2000

The pain in my heart increased each day when I didn't get to see Tri. I thought volunteering with hospice would ameliorate some of the pain and, in a small way, pay back for what they did. With hospice, I was able to visit with patients to give the caregiver a break. Being with the patients brought back lots of memories, but somehow it was cathartic for me. I met a young Vietnamese patient who had liver cancer. He was working at IBM as an engineer, and we used to greet each other in the hallway. I showed him all the tricks I had learned from taking care of my brother, like what food he could eat to keep up with his treatment and always having his pain medications with him. After a few months with hospice, he succumbed to his illness. His death was devastating for his mother - he was the only child. She kept thanking me at the funeral. I didn't know why because I had done nothing for him. I was just a volunteer.

Another patient I met through hospice had breast cancer. The cancer treatment had prevented her from working. During a meeting with hospice, we found out she was about to be evicted from her apartment. I went on my routine visit with her and gave her what I had in my savings account to pay for one month's rent. I saw myself in her shoes just a few years earlier. I met a young mother with a dying baby whom she named Angel. My visit with baby Angel was short lived - she died just a few weeks later. I still prayed for that baby. Every Saturday, I visited a certain hospice patient in a nursing home. He didn't talk at all, but he enjoyed the chocolate I brought with me each visit. Seeing patients in the nursing home was more taxing emotionally. Loneliness and sadness pervaded at every turn in the nursing homes. During the time with hospice, I was able to see a broad spectrum of ages and a plethora of illnesses. Disease didn't discriminate - sex, age, or race. The experience I went through with Tri engendered courage to see the end of life for these patients as a new journey. Hospice was a compassionate means for those who had to face the end-of-life sojourn. The way they cared for patients was inspiring. My family had great respect and appreciation for hospice.

Back at IBM, the pain that I carried in my heart had a negative impact on my performance. I thought long and hard about how to mitigate this pain. Eventually, I concluded I would become a physician. The experience I had with Tri truly inspired and motivated me to pursue medicine. It would help me to be a more compassionate and sympathetic doctor. It would take two years of night school to finish my prerequisites for medical school, and by then, I would be thirty-three years old. I wasn't sure it would be feasible at my age to go back to school, but I knew becoming a doctor would be cathartic and therapeutic for me. I met up with a counselor at UT to ask her for her advice about my plan of returning to medical school. After reviewing my school records, she didn't think I would be accepted to medical school. I was older, my science background was insufficient, and my grades were poor. She had seen students with better credentials who didn't make it. She knew what impossibilities were, and I didn't. Her advice didn't deter me from achieving my goal. I just needed one school to see me beyond my grades; then I could try to show them what possibilities were with God's help.

While preparing for medical school, I moved back in with Champ so I couldn't be distracted. Teresa and I were drifting apart while she was pursuing her doctorate and I was busy taking care of Tri. When I went back to medical school, she and I decided to go our separate ways. Our relationship had deteriorated to the point of no return, and it was all because of me. I was young, immature, and not very astute. I had wronged Teresa in so many ways in our relationship. My only hope was that she would forgive me.

The day I took my MCAT (Medical College Admission Test) was also the day I discovered panic disorder. As soon as the door of the auditorium closed, I felt my heart pounding. My breathing was fast, I felt doomed, and I had to escape out of the auditorium. I asked the test conductor to let me out, and she had to stop the test and wait for me. I felt embarrassed, and I didn't know what was wrong with me. The MCAT

A Runaway Teenager

was the most formidable test; it was designed to pick out the cream of the crop - rightfully so. Despite that torturous test, performing substandard in the MCAT didn't mean one couldn't become a physician.

My scores came back, and they weren't exactly what I wanted. I retook the test, but the scores didn't change much. As I began my application process to medical school, I was asked to write a personal statement as to why I wanted to become a physician. One late evening in my office at IBM, I was writing my personal statement. When I began to relive what happened to Tri, tears streamed down my face with each stroke on the keyboard. I had to stop typing and run out of my office when the tears were forming a puddle on the keyboard. I didn't cry that much except a little on the very first day when Tri died, even though that was brief. Perhaps the guilty feeling came over me because I wish there were more I could have done to save Tri. I was willing to give Tri any part of my body to pay for anything that could give him a chance. When I finished my personal statement, which took a few weeks, I applied to medical schools. Unfortunately, I wasn't invited to attend. I knew what my problems were, but a solution was more important.

My research showed that there were foreign medical schools in Poland, India, and even Russia. I loved the idea, but they were too far from America. I found a Caribbean medical school in Dominica. The criticism on the internet about foreign medical schools was ferocious and discouraging. Most people seemed to agree that foreign medical schools were easy to get in but hard to get out. Nevertheless, there were positive comments and success stories as well. I amassed all the success stories I could find and let those stories be my inspiration.

With that spirit, I applied to Ross University School of Medicine in Dominica and was accepted for the fall semester of 2000. I was elated and ready to start medical school, but I wasn't able to borrow the money for it. The financial aid office informed me I had forty thousand dollars in credit card debt that needed to dissolve before allowing me to borrow money. I prayed that if God wanted me to become a doctor, he would find a way for me.

I went to the bank for help, but they couldn't lend me that much money. As I was walking out of the bank, a sign was advertising for a home equity loan. I had no idea what it was. Upon further inquiry, the bank manager explained that if I had any money in my home, I could borrow from it. My home was located in an impoverished part of town, something was always broken, and I didn't think it would be worth much in value. I didn't want to bother him, but he insisted that I allow him to look at the home. To my surprise, I was able to borrow enough money to dissolve all my credit card debt. I quickly contacted the financial aid office to notify them of my latest economic situation. The financial aid office was impressed, but I still had to have a co-signer for at least the first year. If I wanted to make it to school on time, I had to figure out a solution for this new problem. I knew very well about this co-signer conundrum. The last time my boss co-signed for me, he and his wife almost got a divorce. I didn't want anyone to face such a quandary, but I had to have someone help me for one year.

The only person who could understand and knew my goals was Champ. It took me a couple of days before I went to Champ for help. I prayed that Champ wouldn't be upset with me for putting him in such imbroglio. Champ had had a bad experience with co-signing loans for people. His apprehension was understandable. He was about to be responsible for twenty thousand dollars. Champ was supportive of my goal - he signed the loan for me. I promised him I would pay his loan off first when I made it through medical school. My boss at IBM tried to convince me that my future would be better if I stayed with the company. I was grateful for my boss's advice, but I wanted to start my healing process.

My family had become self-sufficient and no longer needed me to help them. My siblings continued to improve their lives as productive citizens. My oldest sister and her husband worked day and night to save enough money to move their kids out of the housing project to a beautiful home in the suburbs. Mark, my oldest brother, was able to find a job with an electronic company and moved on with his life. My last sister in Viet Nam, Mary, made it to America with her husband and kid. Nick graduated from the University of Texas in Austin with an electrical engineering degree. My little sister, Lindsay, who had motion sickness with each bus ride when she first came to America, graduated from the Texas State University at San Marcos with a BA degree and worked for IBM. Eventually, Lindsay found her calling and went back to school and became a registered nurse. Although her road to becoming a nurse was daunting, she never gave up or gave in to achieve her goals. My youngest brother graduated with a chemical engineering degree from the University of Texas in Austin, and he ended up working for a chemical company. My cousin Harold was also moving on with his life.

In August, I said goodbye to family and friends and headed for Dominica. I flew to Miami and from Miami to Puerto Rico, then a propeller plane to Dominica. The last stretch was a challenge for some of us. To get to the landing strip, the pilot had to get over the mountain then drop quickly to land the plane on the short landing strip, which ended in the ocean. Although I didn't hear any stories about a plane landing in the sea, I always prayed that the break was good every time we landed in Dominica.

Dominica was a third-world country, and the airport displayed its desperate economy. When one student didn't like what she saw at the airport, she turned around and returned home. Most of us were committed to this journey; we couldn't just turn back from our goals. The trip from the airport to our campus was another challenge for some of us. The kamikaze transporters, as we nicknamed them, and the winding road created such havoc

A Runaway Teenager

on those who couldn't handle motion sickness. I realized that the escape on the boat for five nights and four days incidentally prepared me for this. My driver had to stop for some students to take a break before continuing to our campus.

The road to our campus was alluring. Some of the students in the van weren't enjoying the view and probably were cursing the kamikaze driver silently. These students were far away from home for the first time in a third-world country. I was sympathetic and inspired to see my peers express such determination to achieve their dreams and looked forward to our camaraderie. The smell of the ocean, the coconut trees standing tall on the seashore, the sound of the crashing waves, and the gentle wind caressing my face brought me back to Galang once again. I could see a little boy frolicking in the beach half-naked every afternoon, running back to the barracks to eat spam for dinner. I couldn't believe that little boy was going to medical school.

Ross University School of Medicine was in Portsmouth, Dominica. The island didn't have many tourists, but its boiling lakes were one of the attractions. The people in Dominica were proud to call their island "the nature island." My fall class of 2000 was approximately three hundred students.

Living in a third-world country was strenuous for those who hadn't seen such countries. Within a few weeks, approximately five percent went home. More dropped out after each semester. At least thirty percent disappeared by the fourth semester. For those who were all in, we settled in with the housing available to us. I found a small cottage that was sitting on four cinder blocks right across from campus. There was no hot water. The electricity went off at the end of the month, right before our exams, so I studied by candlelight. The library had a generator, but it wasn't big enough for all the students. When the library closed at night, we walked home together for our safety. The coffee shop on campus was essential. There was an empty field where students played soccer frequently. They were entertaining - more so than the basketball players. The Catholic students used one of the classrooms for Sunday mass, and our psychiatry professor was our deacon. The movie nights were also in one of the classrooms. We were creative with our entertainment.

Our classroom lectures started at eight and lasted until five or a little later. When the lectures were done, I continued my studies until midnight or later. These routines were similar for most medical students. I seldom missed classes because they were necessary for my learning. The majority of our professors were great teachers who were dedicated to their teaching. I stayed away from the negative talk about the school and focused on my studies. There was lots of criticism about foreign medical schools on the World Wide Web. We didn't need to add more fuel to the fire. Those of us who were focusing on our studies were able to achieve our goals.

During the two years in medical school, I met a group of people who became my lifelong friends. We did almost everything together, from going to classes to eating dinner at Seaside Cafe every day. If someone didn't show up for dinner, we would worry. At dinner, we talked, laughed, and ignored our schoolwork for at least a few minutes. Most of us left our loved ones behind to pursue this dream, and our friendship and camaraderie were the best things to keep our sanity.

At the end of each semester, I came home to visit the family and recharge for the following semester, but some students stayed on the island for the whole two years. By the fourth semester, I developed irritable bowel syndrome (IBS) with bad bloating and acid reflux. My anxiety about my IBS was causing so much stress that I met with a psychiatrist in our school, and he diagnosed me with generalized anxiety disorder. I was told that my anxiety was the cause of my IBS. I flew home for further medical evaluation right before the final exam. I wasn't sure if I could pass the fourth semester because of my illness, but I took all my studying materials to study while I was home. I saw a gastroenterologist about my bloating and acid reflux, and he said that I had a motility disorder that felt in the line of IBS. He explained that it was due to stress I had in medical school. I came back to school to finish my fourth semester. Our group made it off the "Rock" after completing four semesters. I couldn't believe that I passed everything. We would do our third and fourth years in America. God was with me, as always.

I wasn't the only one experiencing issues because of the stress. I met an upperclassman who stopped studying for two weeks because he was so stressed from studying for eight to ten hours a day that he couldn't open a book again. A friend of mine developed stroke-like symptoms in the middle of the night. Other students had similar anxiety, and we called ourselves the GAD (generalized anxiety disorder) group. It was complicated for people to understand panic and anxiety disorders unless they had it. In the GAD group, we knew and understood each other perfectly, and our support for each other was perdurable. Psalm 46:1–3 helped me in these troubled times. I shared it with the group whenever possible: "God is our refuge and strength, an ever-present help in trouble. Therefore we will not fear, though the earth give way and the mountains fall into the heart of the sea, though its waters roar and foam and the mountains quake with their surging." Our friendship grew closer with each semester. I wouldn't have made it without their support.

Coming back to America was a thrill for me. I was halfway through my goals, yet I felt so humble. Some students had to stay back because they weren't able to complete the fourth semester. We were fortunate to be back on American soil safely after two exhausting years. We were eager to start our fifth semester in Miami.

Chapter 14

The American Dream

October 2004

After a short visit with my family, I needed to find my way to Miami for our fifth semester. My youngest brother was kind enough to give me his eleven-year-old Toyota Celica. I was very grateful for the car, and I didn't care how old it was. I wasn't concerned about the possibility of its problems on the long journey from Texas to Miami because I was relying solely on God to protect me through my journey.

After two and a half days of eight to ten hours each day of driving, I made it to Miami without an incident. I loved Miami. Cuban coffee was our daily energy drink. I ate at Pollo Tropical, a Cuban fast-food chain, daily because it was cheap and tasted fantastic. The library at the Florida International University in Miami was our new home for the fifth semester.

One night when I was studying in my apartment, I felt pain in my chest that radiated to my jaw. I thought I was having a heart attack. I called up my friends for help. They took me to the emergency room and waited for hours for me. The ER

A Runaway Teenager

physician sent me home and advised me that I had "medical student syndrome." My anxiety and panic disorder had gotten better after the island, but I still had episodic events. When the fifth semester was over, some of us decided to stay in Miami to study for our United States Medical Licensing Examination. I was able to concentrate and passed my first USMLE. When I received my test results, I was on my knees, thanking God for being with me every step of the way. I felt fortunate that my first step to becoming a physician was completed. I drove my Toyota Celica back to Texas without a single hiccup. I was ready for my third and fourth years of medical school.

After a short break to visit my family and friends, I was off to Brooklyn, New York, for my third and fourth years. As with all my rotations, I started with eagerness and enthusiasm to learn and do as much as possible. It didn't matter what rotation I was in, from psychiatry to OB/GYN, I was the first one in and the last one out.

I learned how to place IVs on patients to help out the nurses when they needed me. Arterial blood gas (ABG) was a diagnostic tool reserved for respiratory therapists and physicians. This procedure involved placing a needle into an artery to obtain blood to determine how sick a patient was. I asked the respiratory therapist if she could teach me how. Her schedule was hectic, but if I could get to the hospital at five in the morning, she would teach me. The following day I got up at three thirty and left the house around four so I could get to the hospital right at five for my lessons. She was surprised

I showed up. Other medical students had asked her to teach them, but they never came to learn. After some basic techniques and watching her with a few patients, she allowed me to try on my first patient. When the blood shot back into my syringe as my needle pierced through the artery on the patient's wrist, an overwhelming joy came over me that only a third-year medical student could experience. The respiratory therapist and I were in shock to see that I succeeded on my first try.

The OB/GYN rotation was fun and educational, especially female anatomy, including working in the operating room (OR) as much as we were allowed to. Before a C-section, our professor would ask one of the students to empty the patient's bladder by placing a catheter in the bladder. This procedure was a challenge to many male students and even some female students. We had to insert the catheter into the bladder, and very often, the catheter ended up in the wrong place. We would get a scolding for not knowing our anatomy.

One morning while I was waiting for my turn for a procedure, a nurse came up to me.

"Do you have a girlfriend?" she whispered in my ear. "If you did, you would know how to place that catheter."

I was too stunned to respond, to tell her that although I had had girlfriends, we hadn't done a thorough surface anatomy on each other. Undoubtedly, the techs and nurses in the OR enjoyed watching the students struggle to find a pee hole.

A Runaway Teenager

Another nurse who saw how nervous I was advised me to aim north of the vagina opening below the clitoris, then I would get it. I was grateful for his advice but still uneasy about this part of the female anatomy. When my friend stepped up for her turn, the whole OR was dead silent, and I could hear my heart beating out of my chest. As soon as the urine came through the catheter and drained straight to the bucket on the floor, I could hear a sound of relief from the staff. However, when my friend bent down and picked up the bucket with her sterile glove, I tried to yell out, "No," but it was too late. The attending stopped us from being in the OR that day and gave us a lecture about sterility, which we had had multiple times. We were just nervous. In the OB/GYN clinic, the most fun and rewarding thing for me was doing Pap smears. In this procedure, discovering a cervix became natural to me. By the end of the month, I was doing Pap smears for all the residents. I truly felt I was contributing to patient care.

My internal medicine rotation was the busiest and just as educational. Each medical student was assigned to follow a first-year resident to learn about internal medicine. My resident was seeing about twenty patients a day. He was so busy that he made a skeleton of his progress notes at home and brought them with him the next day to fill out the essential data for each patient. In addition to seeing all the patients, he had to draw blood on each patient every morning for their lab. I volunteered to come in every day at five in the morning to help him with the morning's lab. He couldn't believe I could do the arterial blood gas for all patients in the ICU every morning. In a small way, it gave me great comfort that I was helping to care for the patients. Touching each patient assuaged the pain of losing Tri little by little every day.

At the end of my third year, I was euphoric when I passed my USMLE Step 2. I knew God had a hand in it. By now, most students had an idea of what they wanted to do for their future. Initially, I was interested in looking for a career to put my hands to good use. I loved surgery, but my bladder was too small. I did an elective rotation in anesthesiology, which was enticing for its lifestyle and economic benefits. Ergo, it was a competitive field being pursued by many medical students. I applied for as many anesthesiology programs as I could but didn't get in. I also applied to a one-year program in internal medicine in Tulsa. I was accepted with only one interview. Without a residency and passing all three USMLE exams, I couldn't become a physician, which many foreign graduates feared. God was looking out for me, as always.

When I started my one-year internal medicine residency, I was hoping to reapply for anesthesiology the following year. My first rotation as a resident was in the Intensive Care Unit (ICU). I was intimidated and clueless, but the ICU nurses and the senior physicians were helpful.

On my first day in the ICU, I was standing at the nurse's station, going over a patient's chart, when I heard a voice call

A Runaway Teenager

out "Doctor." I didn't hear the call and continued reading the chart. The voice came again, louder this time, "Doctor." Startled, I looked up to where the voice came from and saw a nurse pointing her finger in my direction. I turned around to look behind my back, and there was no one behind me. The nurse pointed her finger at me multiple times to suggest that she was talking to me. I pointed my finger at my chest to confirm that she wanted me. She shook her head up and down.

Up to that moment, I didn't see myself as a doctor. I was just a medical student the day before, and her call officially terminated my medical student days. Being a foreign graduate and the first Ross student accepted into this program, even for one year, I was determined to make a long-lasting impression for my school so more Ross students could be accepted, requiring assiduity on my part.

My dream of becoming a doctor had finally arrived. My mission was to treat all my patients as if they were my family members. I propelled myself into each rotation with enthusiasm and compassion for my patients. I gave patients as much time as they wished to ask questions, and if I wasn't able to answer the questions, I would consult someone who could.

I was always honest with the patients about their illness. The most stressful thing was to tell a patient's family members that their loved one was going to die, but I was able to share the bad news without the family being upset with me. ICU was commonplace for such situations. On one occasion, a young woman was found to have an ischemic bowel, and there was nothing that could help her after a few days in ICU. All the clinical and medical indications implied that she wasn't going to make it until the morning. The family was in shock because everything happened so quickly. The patient was having dinner with them, and the next thing they knew, she was in the ICU. My job was to share the grimmest news to the family, that the patient may not make it until the morning, so that they could say their goodbyes.

I remembered how hard it was to say goodbye to Tri. I wasn't sure if I was capable of telling the patient's family this bad news. When I walked to the family room, and as soon as I made eye contact with the family, tears were rolling down my face, and they knew it was bad news. I shared the news with them. We all cried together. They thanked me for my care. But most importantly, they realized it was difficult for me to give bad news to the family. My experience with Tri had taught me the importance of delivering bad news with compassion.

We were always trained to take the nurses' calls with urgency. Every time I was paged by a nurse, whether the issue seemed critical or not, I addressed the problem as soon as possible. We were taught to take patients' complaints seriously. This action alone had saved lives and complications for many patients. If we could appease the nurses, the night was peaceful. If not, we would pay for it. I would be forever grateful for their help through the most demanding year as an intern.

A Runaway Teenager

As the year got closer to the end, I reapplied for an anesthesiology residency and hoped for better luck the second time around. But God had a different plan for me.

A few months before my residency ended, Dr. W - my program director - offered me a full residency in internal medicine, and I took it. I was so appreciative of his offer and promised him I would give my best to complete this residency. If Dr. W hadn't given me that job, I'm not sure where I would have ended up. Appreciation wasn't a word big enough to describe how grateful I was to Dr. W. At the end of my first year of residency, I was surprised when I was awarded the most compassionate intern of the year, an award I didn't even know existed.

When my first year was over, I was no longer an intern. I became a senior with responsibility for two interns. We did our best to prevent any unacceptable outcomes for our patients. We were responsible for approximately ten to fifteen patients each day, sometimes more, depending on how busy the hospital was. I knew this volume didn't compare to what residents carried in other programs, but University of Oklahoma at Tulsa Internal Medicine undeniably molded us to be the best physicians to serve our community.

All my attending teachers were always ready to teach and help us whenever we needed them. I tried to show my interns what I learned in my first year so they wouldn't make the same mistakes. Most importantly, I taught them not to be lazy when caring for patients. Laziness would bring bad outcomes.

One of my interns was having the opposite problem. The interns' job was to see all the patients that were assigned to them. After they finished seeing all the patients, they met up with the senior and attending to round on all patients together. Roger was always late for rounds with our boss. My attending was understandably upset and wanted to fail Roger. If Roger failed, I had failed him. I was responsible for teaching my interns. I asked my boss to give me one week to see what Roger was doing so I could fix it. I asked Roger to show me precisely when he left his home to the time he finished seeing all the patients. Roger picked me up at five in the morning at my apartment, and we came to the hospital for his rounds. After observing Roger with a few patients, I knew why he was late.

Roger was bathing, changing bedpans, and making beds for each patient. I told Roger that he had a different role as a physician. He needed to evaluate the patients' medical conditions first. When we finished our rounds with our boss, he could go back to doing all those things for his patients to his desires. I knew Roger was competent and not a lazy resident. His previous training in Kenya made him compassionate, idealistic, and altruistic. I loved him for it. I fought for Roger with all my energy because gossip was getting to everyone in the program. I had seen residents prevaricate to impress the attendings, but Roger had never lied in front of the attendings to impress them.

When the truth was known and shown, Roger was able to move on to his second year. By the time Roger made it to his third year, the morning round was a one-person show. The attending stepped aside and watched Roger round with residents. He did so well that one of the attendings wanted to know who his senior was. I was so glad that I was able to fight for Roger. I was so proud and happy that our attendings saw Roger for who he truly was - a great person and an exceptional physician.

After my second year of residency, I passed my USMLE Step 3, and this was the last examination for me to become a physician officially. God was there for me. I also graduated from OU-Tulsa internal medicine residency with the "superior humanistic attributes and professionalism" of the year award. This was a surprise to me. I was interested in becoming a wound care physician in my second year of residency. However, there wasn't a wound care job available when I graduated.

I took a job working in the ER as a night doctor while waiting for an opportunity to do wound care. I worked twelve shifts a month. My shift started on Friday nights from five in the afternoon to seven in the morning and seven o'clock in the evening to seven in the morning for Saturdays and Sundays. Working in the ER as a nocturnist was emotionally and physically burdensome for me, but it was an invaluable experience nonetheless.

As internal medicine physicians, we usually would see patients after the ER physicians saw them. I saw patients as soon as they were off the gurney from the ambulance. I had to diagnose their problems, then admit the patients to the hospital. The rewards came when I was able to stabilize the acute illnesses.

Artist: Sudipta Steve Dasgupta

A Runaway Teenager

Occasionally, I had to tell the patients and their families a dreadful diagnosis. Mr. S came to my ER with severe abdominal pain. While waiting for the abdominal CT scan to complete, I tried to manage his pain and low blood pressure. This was an ominous sign. A few minutes later, I had an urgent call from the radiologist that Mr. S had an abdominal aortic dissection - the wall of his abdominal aorta was being separated. The dissection was long and extensive. A vascular surgeon on call was consulted immediately. In the meantime, Mr. S was losing blood very rapidly. I ordered a rapid transfusion for him.

"I can't save him," the vascular surgeon said to me after he looked at the CT scan. "He is going to die."

"Could you please inform the family of your diagnosis?" I insisted.

"No. You do it, Ha." He refused and walked away.

The diagnosis reminded me of Tri. I was devastated for the family. Arguing with the surgeon wouldn't change his mind. Besides, I would do a better job of giving the news to the family. My nurse accompanied me to talk to the family. The family was patiently waiting for what I had to say about their father.

"I am so sorry. There was nothing we could do to help your father." We all cried. "Please come and spend as much time with him as you can because when I turn off the transfusion, Mr. S will go quickly," I sobbed.

"We appreciate you for taking care of him, and we know it must be difficult for you," one of the members of the family said out loud.

"I can honestly say that I know how you feel." I wiped my tears and said goodbye to them.

I could never forget the day we said goodbye to Tri. Now this family had to face the inevitable - saying goodbye to a loved one forever. A short time after the transfusion was off, Mr. S's monitor showed a flat line - he passed away. I went back to my desk, and my heart was dilated with misery, but I had eight more patients waiting for my undivided attention.

We saw various cases in the ER, including complex situations, unexpected situations, and amusing situations. Mrs. J came into the ER one night with a main complaint of being unable to urinate.

"You are a handsome doctor," she stated while I was interviewing her. Her comment made me turn red because I had not been accused of that for a long time. My head was getting big.

"She's blind, doctor," her granddaughter said, turning to me. You just never knew what you were going to get when you worked night shifts in the ER.

Two months after working in the ER, I found a wound care job in Muskogee, Oklahoma, about a one-hour drive from my home in Tulsa. It was an opportunity for me to start my wound care career. I continued my nocturnist job in Tulsa on the weekends and drove to Muskogee on Monday morning when I finished my Sunday night shift. The wound care job in Muskogee was Monday to Friday. When I finished my Friday in Muskogee, I drove straight to the ER in Tulsa to begin my night shift at five o'clock in the afternoon. The most challenging thing was to drive to Muskogee on Monday morning after being up all night, but the Rockstar energy drinks helped. Wound care was not as glamorous as other medical fields - it could be noisome at times. However, if one could tolerate the foul, odorous wound, the reward was exuberant.

By the time I graduated from medical school, I had three hundred thousand dollars in student loans, and the interest began to accumulate. I searched high and low for a way to manage my finances. I met multiple financial advisors, read many books, and listened to quite a few radio financial shows. However, the only cogent advice I found was to pay off my debt as soon as possible and live as if I was a resident or a pauper until I was debt free. I championed the concept and began a journey to financial freedom.

I continued to live in my apartment and worked two full-time jobs. The most pressing debt for me to pay off was the loan that Champ co-signed for me. To fulfill my promise to Champ, I paid off his loan promptly with my first few paychecks. I knew Champ was worried because he was receiving a loan reminder every month. When his loan was paid off, I called and let him know that because of him, I made it through medical school.

Besides the school debt, I wanted to pay back all the loans that I had borrowed or had been given by friends. I couldn't forget all those who had helped me, especially what Mr. and Mrs. Howard did for me with the airplane tickets for my family to come to America. As soon as I could save up seven thousand dollars, I drove home to Austin and invited Mr. and Mrs. Howard to a steak dinner to give them back the money they gave me. Unquestionably, they didn't expect me to give back the money because it was a gift. During the dinner, Mrs. Howard was discussing the economy and their financial standing. I reminded them of what they did for my family, and I would always be grateful for their kindness. To ensure their generosity wasn't taken for granted, I asked them to allow me to give back the money they gave me, and they accepted. Those who had given me money or lent me money, I looked them up and requited all the money with interest. All my friends who had helped me emotionally and financially, I owed them an eternal debt.

I was content living in an apartment while I paid off my debt, but one morning when I came home from work, my apartment was burglarized, and all valuable things were taken. I was upset and felt violated. I wanted to have a beer to calm me down, but even the beer was stolen - this upset me the most. I laughed about it with my friends. Immediately, I purchased a home and moved out of the apartment a few months later. Although this move stalled my progress to being debt free, my apartment was no longer safe.

Chapter 15

A Family of My Own

July 2014

While I was living in Tulsa, my brother Stanley made his usual trips to see his in-laws in Oklahoma City. I knew Stanley's in-laws to a certain extent. I met Vivian, Stanley's wife's younger sister, a few years before medical school. It was a wonderful visit, and I enjoyed meeting everyone in Stanley's wife's family. It had been a long while since I last saw Vivian. When I was taking one of my breaks from medical school, I took her to see a doctor because she wasn't feeling well. Now Vivian was married with a two-year-old boy - Ethan. When I met Ethan, he ran to me and kissed my hand. I fell in love with him. Vivian and I kept in touch, and we talked a few times after our visit. By then, we had fallen hard for each other.

Artist: Sudipta Steve Dasgupta

A Family of My Own

We dated for five years, and I proposed to Vivian on July 4th, 2014. It was an exciting night for us. Our friends brought tons of fireworks, and we had a dance floor in our backyard with loudspeakers for the party. Vivian was suspicious about the party, but she still cried copiously when I went down on my knee to ask her for her hand in marriage. After caring for many people for so long, I had no desire to have children, but if children happened, it would be God's will. Vivian was content with no additional children. She accepted my proposal. We married a year later. Vivian, Ethan, and my mother-in-love moved to live with me in Fort Smith, Arkansas.

Two years into our marriage, we were pregnant with my first child at fifty years old, and I knew God had a plan for us. Vivian's health was uneventful except for occasional nausea and vomiting during the nine months of pregnancy. I took Vivian to the hospital the day of the labor. I waited for her to be situated in her room. After her epidural procedure was completed, I went to the clinic to check on my patients. Fortunately, my clinic was located in the same hospital, just a few steps from the labor and delivery floor.

Around ten in the morning, I was paged because my wife was about to deliver our child. Vivian was trying to push hard, but the baby wasn't moving much. The physician tried different techniques to help Vivian and the baby. Then suddenly, Vivian needed an emergency C-section. She was moved to the operating room, and her C-section began. I was right next to Vivian, praying for her and the baby. We both were crying with fear.

"Lord, I don't care what will happen to me. Please save our baby," Vivian cried into my ear. The greatest fear all my life was to lose a loved one. Losing Tri was the worst pain I had to deal with, and now Vivian and I were facing the possibility of losing Peter. In these darkest moments, I thought of how God had protected me all my life - an epiphany overcame my fear. "God will save Peter, Love," as I whispered firmly into her ear, putting my head against hers. A few minutes went by; I heard the physician yelling out for another physician for help. By now, the operating room was full of staff and observers as I looked up, hoping to see the paged physician. The operator was paging another physician to our room multiple times.

Vivian and I began to cry even more because we knew there was something wrong. Another few minutes went by, there were no signs of the paged physician, but a family physician was rounding with his residents. Vivian's doctor asked him to help her take the baby out because he was stuck. Within a few minutes, he was able to remove Peter from the womb. Peter was transferred to an incubator about ten feet from us. Vivian and I were crying even more now because Peter wasn't crying. I don't know how long it was before Peter made his first cry, but it was an eternity for us.

Peter's cry was the sweetest sound for us. We cried even harder now because we were so happy to hear our baby cry. I made a promise to myself that I would always cherish his cries, even in the middle of the night. Peter was moved to the Neonatal

Intensive Care Unit (NICU), and Vivian returned to her room. She was finally able to get some rest. I decided to swing by NICU to visit Peter before I went back to the clinic. Seeing Peter through the windows with all the monitor devices on his body made me love Vivian and Peter even more. I knew God had answered our prayers. The clinic was canceled by the time I walked through the door. The staff had heard the PA and figured Vivian was in trouble, so they canceled the clinic to give me a chance to be with my family.

Vivian was mildly awake when I made it back to her room. The wound on her abdomen started to bleed with bright red blood. The surgeon determined that she had a bleeder, and it needed to be corrected in the operating room. It was crushing news to Vivian, but she knew the bleeding needed to be stopped. Around midnight Vivian made it out of the operating room. The surgeon found the bleed and fixed it. We were glad that problem was resolved for now. The following day she developed high fevers and chills. Additional workup needed to be done to figure out this new development. Vivian was rationally frustrated, but we knew the most complicated step was completed, and our Peter was getting better daily.

On the third day, Vivian wanted to go home even though she still had a fever. On the same day, Peter was refusing his oxygen - he kept pulling off the oxygen tube in his nose. The nurses were so annoyed by his resolve that they kept the oxygen off him. Peter and Vivian had a unique way of communicating with

A Runaway Teenager

each other. They wanted to be closer to each other at home. We went home the next day. Vivian's fever eventually subsided. Peter was happy to be home with us. Everyone - grandparents, aunts, uncles, and cousins - was in my tiny duplex to be with Peter. My love for Vivian, Ethan, and Peter grew stronger with each heartbeat of mine. What happened in that operating room deepened my commitment to love and care for my family for the rest of my life. God had given me more than I deserved.

When I began my career in wound care, I wanted to have a job other than internal medicine, but it became the second love of my life, after my wife. A few years into wound care, I could save limbs that I didn't think could be saved. My love for wound care grew with each wound that I healed. Wound care required patience and kindness to be able to help this type of patient. Some wounds could take months and even years to heal. I would do my very best to help to save each limb.

All the patients who walked through the door in my clinic, whether they had money or not, got exceptional care and respect from me. The population of patients that I saw in my clinic was primarily poor. Some of them couldn't come because they didn't have money for gasoline for their cars. Some even asked to make payments on what they owed me. I always told them to ignore my bills. I didn't want my patients to lose their limbs because they couldn't afford a few hundred dollars. It wasn't too long ago that I was poor and broken - I could empathize with my patients.

The majority of the patients who came to our clinic found that our clinic was vibrant and fun. We were family to them. When the patients became close to me, it would be a problem. The patients were used to seeing me weekly. So when I was sick for a while, they wouldn't come to see another wound physician until I was back in the office. We had lots of laughs, though there were some tears when I had to give the patient bad news. I treated the patients as if they were my family members. In that way, they would always receive the best care.

I tried to inculcate the same values to my medical students in hopes that I could influence them to care for the patients the way I did. Being a wound care physician helped heal my wound. When I lost my brother Tri over twenty years earlier, I had a deep wound in my heart that I didn't think could be healed. With each wound I healed, I felt my wound was healing a little with it. Over fourteen years of doing wound care, my wound improved. Whenever I saw Tri in my dreams, I no longer woke up with tears. My patients had helped me heal my wound, but they didn't know what they had done for me. I was so grateful to them for allowing me to help them. God had guided me to do wound care because He knew ultimately it would heal my wound.

Although my life was tumultuous, it has been a wonderful life. God was carrying me on his shoulders through all challenges because those weren't my footprints. He knew what I needed and when I needed it. Without those challenges, I wouldn't be the person I am today - a little more caring, a little more giving, and a little more loving. I am so grateful for America, a promised land. Without it, my family and I couldn't have had the life we have. My running away days are over. I will continue to live my life - just as I promised God on that fateful day on the ocean - with love.

1 Corinthians 13:4

"Love is patient, love is kind. It does not envy, it does not boast, it is not proud. It does not dishonor others, it is not self-seeking, it is not easily angered, it keeps no record of wrongs. Love does not delight in evil but rejoices with the truth. It always protects, always trusts, always hopes, always perseveres."

Acknowledgements

Writing the acknowledgments page meant I had finished my book. I knew there was a hand in it to help me to complete this arduous task - God. The editing and proofreading were completed. And now my last task was to finish this page to bring my story to its dénouement. Over the years, the people who were inquisitive about my life would always advise me to put my journey on paper. Obviously, my family and loved ones, who know me well, also encouraged me to share my story. Of course, my son Ethan would ask me to tell him stories about me whenever I had a chance to put him to bed. My wife would tell Ethan how bad I had it so he would be a better son - typical guilt-trip parenting and I loved it. After Peter was born in 2017, I wrote down a goal to finish my book in 2020. My only hope was that my children would be able to learn from what I went through to better their lives.

One night after Mother's Day weekend in 2020, I decided to write one paragraph each night to see how far it would take me. I wrote mostly when I was on the Stairmaster, using my phone about ninety minutes each time. To keep it a surprise for my wife and everyone in the family, I didn't write when I was at home with them. Sometimes when I had a break between patient care, I would write as much as I could. When the first draft was done, I hired a publishing company to help me with the editing and to publish my book. A year later, the manuscript was completed. The excitement and happiness just weren't enough to describe how I feel to have accomplished this goal.

For sure, I couldn't have written this book without God's help. I am so blessed for what He has done for me. He carried me on his shoulders throughout my life and still does. Whatever I have accomplished in my life, it's because of God.

My parent's love was immeasurable. My mother is an inspiration for our family. She sacrificed all her life for all her children. A single mother without an education, living in poverty, with a bunch of kids to care for, she demanded us to be the best we could. I love you more than you know and am very thankful for never giving up the fight for your children. My siblings, Harold, brothers-in-love, and sisters-in-love, you all have done a great job of becoming productive citizens. You have created a wonderful life for your families so your children will have the opportunity to pursue the American dream. I am proud and appreciative of what you have done with your lives.

My uncle who brought me to America. You are the person who started my journey in Austin. Without this start, I wouldn't be the Texan I am today. I am truly sorry for the pain I had caused. I love you and am indebted to you for my incipience in America.

When I had nowhere to go, my "adopted" mother sheltered me and gave me a chance that would change the course of my future. A white lady with three kids, living paycheck to paycheck, and whom I asked to give me a few days when I ran away, she gave me two and half years - my "adopted" family. I will never forget your generosity. I love you.

The people whom I had encountered through my years of growing up made a great impact in my life. The programmers, engineers, colleagues, and all the bosses at IBM who created a special place in their lives for me. The friends who had helped me through my difficult years prior to the arrival of my family and when I was taking care of Tri and my family. I will always remember your kindness as long as I live.

The staff, nurses, doctors at Brackenridge Hospital and Hospice of Austin who gave Tri the best care, our family owes you a debt of gratitude.

Medical school years were the most difficult years of my life, and I am not sure I would have made it without my friends. Throughout the vicissitudes of our journey, you were always there for me when I needed you the most. I cherish your friendship with all my heart.

I am a better doctor today because of the attendings at Tulsa-OU Internal Medicine program, whose dedication often went unnoticed and unappreciated. To pay forward for what you have done for me, I will continue to inculcate my students and residents to care for patients the way you taught me.

My life would be incomplete without my lovely wife. She brought joy and happiness that I didn't know existed. Vivian has done an impossible job of keeping our home intact and functional while taking care of our children when I am away most nights of the week. You are my heart. You are my soul. And I can't live without one or the other. I am thankful for the love and support from my in-loves (not in-laws), including my parents, sisters, and brothers. Our lives would be miserable without them.

This book would be hard to complete without the help of Lacey Teague, my personal nurse. Because I wanted this book to be a surprise to my wife and family, I asked Lacey to be my beta reader whenever I finished a paragraph. Additionally, to be able to make our deadline, Lacey had communicated every detail in the book with the artist overseas night and day to illustrate what I think was essential to the readers. The product truly conveyed what a great job she did. I can't thank Lacey enough for going beyond her duty in helping me with this venture.

The artist who brought my story to the surface - Sudipta Steve Dasgupta. When I found Steve, he was dealing with the death of his mother from COVID-19, and he was sick with the disease himself. I felt his pain in my heart and just wanted him to recover from his illness; I would find another artist for the project. Nevertheless, while recovering from the virus, mourning his mother's death, and caring for his brother who also contracted the ailment, Steve graciously accepted our proposal even with a very short timeline to complete the project. When I looked at his paintings, an old adage came through - "A picture is worth a thousand words." Steve was able to articulate my feelings through his art masterfully. I am grateful you gave me your time when you were under insurmountable stress and honored to have your artwork in my book.

A special thanks to my staff in the clinic whose dedication is often glossed over. You have done more for our patients than you can imagine. I don't take your hard work for granted.

For all those patients who have entrusted me to heal your wounds, you have empowered me with a remedy that attenuated my own wound even though you may not know it. This is a gift I can never repay. I love you all.

A final shout-out to the Paper Raven Books publishing team for helping me publish this book. Especially, Morgan Gist MacDonald, whose book - *Start Writing Your Book Today* - gave me the courage to achieve my goal. Kate Allyson and Joy Xiang have done a fantastic job of editing and proofreading, respectively, to bring my book to its fruition. I appreciate everyone in the team for helping me in this new adventure.

I try my best to include everyone in this acknowledgment. Those who feel that I have been remiss in my appreciation, and you have been involved in my life one way or the other, please know that the honor is all mine.

www.ingramcontent.com/pod-product-compliance
Lightning Source LLC
Chambersburg PA
CBHW030908080526
44589CB00010B/202